FIRE IN THE SOUL

100 POEMS FOR HUMAN RIGHTS

FIRE IN THE SOUL

100 POEMS FOR HUMAN RIGHTS

EDITED BY
Dinyar Godrej

NewInternationalist

Fire in the Soul: 100 poems for human rights.

First published in the UK in 2009 by
New Internationalist™ Publications Ltd
Oxford OX4 1BW
www.newint.org
New Internationalist is a registered trademark.

This selection and additional material © Dinyar Godrej / New Internationalist.
Individual poems © The Authors and rights holders.
For detail on copyright and permissions, see Acknowledgements, page 175.

Cover photograph: Selvaprakash L / Drik Picture Library / Majority World.

Designed by Alan Hughes for New Internationalist.

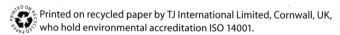 Printed on recycled paper by TJ International Limited, Cornwall, UK,
who hold environmental accreditation ISO 14001.

British Library Cataloguing-in-Publication Data.
A catalogue record for this book is available from the British Library.

Library of Congress Cataloguing-in-Publication Data.
A catalogue record for this book is available from the Library of Congress.

ISBN: 978-1-906523-16-9

Contents

Foreword

INEVITABLY, AND QUITE RIGHTLY, a great deal of the poetry in this anthology amounts to a form of protest. Protest about the denial of human rights; protest about the silencing of human voices. Anyone reading it will respect the urgency of its complaints, and feel moved by the pathos of its situations. But they will also be made to think about the way in which good poetry acts on situations, rather than merely reacting to them – about the way formal ingenuities and imaginative arrangements allow the sorrows, deprivations and atrocities that they describe to be at once particular to their own compelling occasions, and able to seize a general truth about suffering and resilience and survival.

There is always a danger that artifice will not realise these cherished ends, but will instead block or compromise the flow of authentic feeling. That does not happen here. The editor has done his work very well, in choosing pieces where the poets and their translators have also done their work well.

It means that the collection makes an important contribution to the literature of which it forms a part. It is both a landmark and a profoundly involving act of collective witness.

Andrew Motion

Introduction

THE DRIVING IMPULSE of this collection can be traced back to a few torn pages from a library book. I had sought out an anthology of Armenian poetry to look for an older translation of Siamanto's chilling poem 'The Dance'. It's a poem that prefigures the Armenian genocide at the hands of Ottoman Empire forces, which took place while the Western world's attention was focused on the First World War. The poem has lost none of its power to shock and I wondered if earlier translators had given it softer edges. But only a few shreds of paper marked where it had been ripped out.

The Armenian genocide, despite the historical materials available that document it, is still doggedly denied by the Turkish authorities. To accept that it occurred is viewed as an anti-Turkish stance. Turkish writers who have dared explore it have faced harassment – both official and from their more patriotically inclined fellow citizens. It is nearly a hundred years since these terrible events. And yet pages are still being torn out of books by 'concerned citizens', there is no reconciliation and a historical wound is left to fester.

Holding the book in my hands, I knew I had a duty to give this poem another airing, and it appears on page 142.

It is a privilege to present this book under Amnesty International's banner, for it is Amnesty's tireless championing of human rights that informs it. Some of the poets included have read their work in support of Amnesty. Today there are creative people incarcerated, poets among them, simply because they dared to voice their beliefs, and Amnesty will be bringing their plight to the attention of its supporters and getting them to act on their behalf. The organization has also been broadening the scope of its own concern. This anthology proudly showcases poetry related to sexual minorities, which would not have been on the agenda of such an Amnesty collection two decades ago.

After a period in which it had fallen somewhat out of favour, socially and politically engaged poetry is again resurgent. Usually the moment a poem adopts a slogan, or tackles an issue head on, it crumples. The poetry of engagement, like all other poetry, must offer illumination from within. Propaganda or bald protest are garments that don't fit. But can poetry be a potent force in understanding the continual struggle for the social ordering of our lives that we call politics? And can it play its own creative part in that struggle? Of course it can.

In the last few decades there has been a welcome addition to the language of politics – diversity. Although (mis)used equally by the mealy-mouthed and the sincere, the embrace of this term signals a welcome widening of the mainstream. Whereas *realpolitik* remains just as short-sighted and inclined to exclusion, the ideal is now about inclusion, about living with and indeed welcoming the fresh perspectives of difference. Instead of fitting people into moulds, attempting to accommodate them whatever shape they come in: this is still a newish idea for humankind, no matter how many times it may have been voiced in the past.

This rousing collection of poems by an international array of poets, mixing well-known names with relative newcomers, is offered in this spirit. One of these poems started life as a song (Luis Enrique Mejía Godoy's 'Revenge'), one is a recitative ('Rich Woman, Poor Woman') and one even comes from a film script (from the Bosnian film *Perfect Circle*). There are numerous poems in translation which speak with accents that are different from those originally written in English. Certain forms of Arabic and Persian verse are notoriously difficult to translate successfully.

In the last century poetry has gained much in terms of freedom, fluidity and flexibility. An immeasurable wealth of strategies has become available to the poet. But the basic subject of poetry remains both unchanged and endless; it is, above all, an exploration of being. The urge to realize who we are, the journey of becoming and being is at the heart of what we call human rights. Declarations and statutes may use leaden words to define rights, but the areas of human experience they seek to protect are vital. Poetry homes in on this vitality; it can give it a face, a heart and words that linger in the mind. It can offer reflection and nuance, thus creating new ways of looking at what we consider to be our rights.

My effort in this selection is to present poems that can give voice to a range of rights. I chose poems that strive for a direct connection, even when their methods involve indirection. I avoided those that carried too strong a whiff of academe or an overbearing emphasis on craft; such poems can make reading them a chore. By contrast, all these poems ask is for you to start reading. I've resisted grouping them by 'themes' and ranked them by the names of their authors instead in order to let chance provide surprises and unusual juxtapositions.

Rights are too often construed in relation to injustice and the outrages that scar human history. However, in this anthology, alongside the stark and compelling poetry related to genocide, imprisonment, refugees and exile, are poems of assertiveness and hope. A few poems may make you wonder: 'How is this related to human rights?' They are an invitation to think further. The spectrum of voices assembled here address colossal historic events at one end of the scale (such as the Nazi concentration camps in Paul Celan's suffocatingly beautiful 'Deathfugue') and somewhat more domestic concerns at the other (Lorna Goodison's and Rita Ann Higgins' pungent explorations of deprivation). There are poets for whom national identity was of central importance, and there are others for whom the rejection of it was equally vital.

I saw no benefit in leaving obscure or local references unexplained, or the historical context when it mattered to the poem - readers who already possess this knowledge can skip these notes. I hope they do not drown the poems in 'explanation' or stand between the essential requirement of the reader's own engagement needed to make any poem sing.

Here are sparks from the human spirit. May they provide both warmth and light.

Dinyar Godrej

Heavensgate

The other politicos,
privileged by class,
education, family,

preen in their bravado
safe from death, protected by old,
powerful benevolence.

They pay other inmates to sing their praises:
Shouts of 'Baba! Baba! Poor man's saviour'
chase their farts echoing up their own arses.

Other heroes here are men and boys
with no power, no privilege, no class,
nothing to gain: not even a book published.

Their crime is to be poor and proud
in the face of tyranny: unbroken by angels
they worry liars to madness.

And one of these nameless
crawled into my cell at night via sewer pipe
to give me a jar of his own blood

and paper, stolen, inch by inch, hidden up
trained rectums and glued together into
sheets with mango sap.

To take write our suffering

These true heroes are lost
in the heat hazes that shimmer over unmarked
graves riddling the swamp behind the prison walls.

Chris Abani

Chris Abani (born 1966) got into trouble with the Nigerian government when
he was just 18 with the publication of his first novel *Masters of the Board*. The
novel, which revolves around a neo-Nazi takeover of Nigeria, was considered
by the authorities to be incitement to a coup and led to imprisonment in 1985.
Upon his release six months later, he joined a guerrilla theatre group and
soon found himself again in prison. After this jail term, he wrote a play which
earned him a death sentence and a place on death row in Kalakuta Prison.
    The poem above comes from his first book of poems *Kalakuta Republic*
(2001). Abani was freed from Kalakuta in 1991 and lived first in exile in
London, then moved to the United States, where he is currently Professor at
the University of California, Riverside. He has published five novels and four
collections of poetry and his work has won numerous awards.

Cranes in August

They clutter the house,
awkwardly folded, unable
to rise. My daughter makes
and makes them, having heard
the old story: what we create
may save us. I string
a long line of them over
the window. Outside
the gray doves bring
their one vowel to the air,
the same sound
from many throats, repeated.

Kim Addonizio

Kim Addonizio (born 1954) has published four volumes of poetry (with a fifth on its way soon) and a novel. She has also written two instructional books on writing poetry. She conducts workshops in Oakland, California.

This poem was one submitted in reaction to the impending 'shock and awe' attack of Baghdad in 2003. Poet Sam Hamill had been invited to a White House symposium on 'Poetry and the American Voice'. He contacted fellow-poets to send him poems speaking 'for the conscience of our country'. In the space of little over a month 11,000 poets had responded to the call. The resultant website poetsagainstthewar.org continues its mission of 'socially engaged poetry'. The White House symposium got 'postponed'.

A Japanese proverb says that a person who folds 1,000 paper cranes is granted a wish. In 1955 Sadako Sasaki, a 12-year-old Japanese girl who was dying of leukemia as a result of the atomic bomb dropped on Hiroshima, began folding paper cranes from her hospital bed. She and the cranes have since become popular symbols of peace – as also are doves.

from The Desert
(The Diary of Beirut Under Siege, 1982)

1

My era tells me bluntly:
You do not belong.
I answer bluntly:
I do not belong,
I try to understand you.
Now I am shadow
Lost in the forest
Of a skull.

8

We no longer meet,
Rejection and exile keep us apart.
The promises are dead, space is dead,
Death alone has become our meeting point.

9

He shuts the door
Not to trap his joy
…But to free his grief.

10

A newscast
         About a woman in love
         Being killed,
         About a boy being kidnapped
         And a policeman growing into a wall.

12

They found people in sacks:
         One without a head

One without a tongue or hands
One squashed
The rest without names.
Have you gone mad? Please,
        Do not write about these things.

14

There may come a time when you'll be
        Accepted to live deaf and dumb, and perhaps
They'll let you mumble: death,
                Life, resurrection –
            And peace be upon you.

15

He wears Jihad uniform, struts in a mantle of ideas.
A merchant – he does not sell clothes, he sells people.

16

They took him to a ditch and burnt him.
        He was not a murderer, he was a boy.
        He was not…
                He was a voice
Vibrating, scaling the steps of space.
And now he's fluting in the air.

26

A star was drowned in blood,
The blood a boy was talking about
And whispering to his friends:
Only some holes known as stars
Remain in the sky.

27

The night is daylight born black
        On this path.

Sunlight and candlelight are the same
    In the heart's darkness.

32

The cities break up
The earth is a train of dust
Only love
Knows how to marry this space.

33

He is dead. Should I mourn him?
What should I say? Should I say: your life was a word, your death
        its meaning?
Or should I say: the road to the light begins in the forest of
        darkness?

Confusion... They are...
    I hide myself in a cave and close the doors with prayers.

(4 June 1982 – 1 January 1983)

Adonis
Translated from the Arabic by Abdullah al-Udhari

Adonis (Ali Ahmad Said, born 1930) made his mark when just 14 by writing a poem about the newly elected president of Syria which so impressed its subject that he was given a study grant. However, in the 1950s he began to write poetry that not only challenged traditional Arabic forms, but also Syrian society and politics. This led to his imprisonment and his exile in 1956 to Beirut in Lebanon.

He took Lebanese citizenship, but in 1980 emigrated to France to escape the Lebanese civil war. He has been nominated four times for the Nobel Prize for Literature.

This selection is from his long poem 'The Desert' which is in 35 sections and is a *tour de force* evocation of statelessness and loss.

Speaking of Hurricanes

for Micere Mugo and all other African exiles

1

My Sister
have you noticed how
around August/September
every year,

Africa
gathers her storms and
hurls them across the Atlantic to
the poor Americas
and the poorer Caribbean:
Gilbert, Sullivan, Katrina...
blustering, savage, masculine?...

Ow,w,w,...
the ruination they leave behind!
levelled homes
torn cables
poisoned water, and
too many lives snuffed out or at best
broken.

Just reckoning the damage is a
whirlwind of sorts.

And we almost thought:
'how clever of Africa!'

Until we looked around us, and
stopped short on our way to jubilation.

2
See!
Africa had always kept
the more interesting of
the commotions for herself.

Years of economic and political tornadoes
in our courtyards
centuries-old gales that
blew our hopes
up, down, left, right:
anywhere and everywhere… except
forward to fulfilment.

We know tyrannical and despotic
winds that whisked away some of
our ablest bodies and strongest minds to
our conquerors' doorsteps,

where they
cut cane
pick cotton and
reap garbage.

These days, they sit.
African men sit.
Able bodies strong minds and all,
guarding private property or
staring at nothing at all. While

African women in various forms of
civilized bondage are
still and forever wiping
baby snot and adult shit:
bourgeois black or imperial white.

Who cares?!

3

The Slave Trade was only
a chapter, a watershed perhaps, but
really no more than an episode in the hands of
a master tale-performer who knows too well, how
its telling,
its music,
its drums
suit his times.

But speaking of very recent events, my Sister,
have you met any of
the 'post-colonial' African political refugees
shuffling on the streets of
London
Paris
Washington
Stockholm and
The Hague?

Minds – and bodies – discarded
because they tried
to put themselves to good use?

Please,
don't tell me how lucky they are.
They know. We know.
They are the few who got away

...escaped
the secret governments and
their secret cabinets,

the secret cabinets and
their secret agendas for
the secret meetings out of which come
secret decisions, laws, decrees, orders from
secret army to secret police for
secret arrests
secret torture and
secret death.

4

Ow, my Sister, let me lament
my openly beautiful land and her people
who hide good things and bad so well,
only decay and shame become
public,
international.

All storms are dangerous.

But I fear most
the ones I can't see
whose shrieking winds are
not heard around the world
            and
the havoc they wreak
cannot even be discussed.

Ama Ata Aidoo

Ghanaian novelist, playwright and poet **Ama Ata Aidoo** (born 1942) has often
written of the tension between Western and African worldviews. She is a strong
advocate of women's contribution to the African continent, a contribution that
is often overlooked. She has held academic posts and was Ghana's Minister of
Education in the early 1980s, a post she resigned after 18 months.

On the political themes in her writing she says: 'I do have a politicized
imagination. Whatever I write about, sooner or later, has something political in
it. This is true of everything, because the political is basic to human life.'

Epilogue

If this country ever should decide
To dedicate a monument to me

I would accept that honour only
On condition the memorial stands

Not by the sea where I was born –
All my ties with the sea are broken –

Nor by the pine stump in the Tsar's garden
Where a sad ghost still looks for me

But here, where I stood for three hundred hours
Outside these gates that never opened once,

In case in blissful death I might perhaps
Forget the rumbling of those Black Marias

Or how the hated door banged shut against
An old woman howling like an animal.

Then let the melting flakes flow down
Over bronze eyelids as if they were tears,

And may a prison dove coo in the distance
While the ships on the Neva sail quietly on.

Anna Akhmatova
Translated from the Russian by Elaine Feinstein

Little Slave Narrative #1: Master

He would order the women to pull up their clothes
'in Alabama style', as he called it. He would whip them

for not complying. He taught bloodhounds
to chase down negro boys, hence the expression

'hell-hounds on my trail'. He was fond of peach brandy,
put ads in the paper: *Search high, search low*

for my runaway Isaac, my runaway Joe,
his right cheek scarred, occasioned by buckshot,

runaway Ben Fox, very black, chunky made,
two hundred dollars live, and if dead,

bring his dead body, so I may look at it.

Elizabeth Alexander

Elizabeth Alexander (born 1962) is a poet, essayist and playwright raised
in Washington, DC. She has published five books of verse and was selected
to read at Barack Obama's Presidential inauguration in 2009. She currently
teaches in the Department of African American Studies at Yale University.

Anna Akhmatova (1889-1966) is one of Russian poetry's giants. Her work was
suppressed during the Stalinist terror and she endured great hardship. However,
her poetry circulated underground and in later years limited portions of her
work were allowed to be published by the Soviets. Her son spent his youth in
Stalin's gulags and she even resorted to writing poems in praise of Stalin to try
and secure his release.

The poem on the facing page is part of the Epilogue of Akhamatova's
great long poem *Requiem*, which she began writing when her son Lev was
incarcerated and describes her waiting in line outside the Kresty prison. She
herself was under supervision at the time and each lyric from this sequence had
to be committed to memory as soon as it was written and the physical evidence
of its composition destroyed.

The Story of a City

A blue city
Dreamt of tourists
Shopping day after day.

A dark city
Hates tourists
Scanning cafés with rifles.

Samih al-Qasim
Translated from the Arabic by Abdullah al-Udhari

Samih al-Qasim (born 1939) is a Palestinian Druze poet and citizen of Israel. He has been imprisoned several times for his advocacy of Palestinian rights and opposition to government policies, starting in 1960 for his refusal to serve in the Israeli army. He works as a journalist in Haifa.

Nazm

O the one who hides in the mountain of unfamiliarity!
O you that sleep in the quietness of the pearl.
O who remains in memories!
Bring the memories of transparent water.
In a river like forgetfulness, my mind is full of dust.
The voice that comes from the mountain makes me think
That from the one who destroys, how can you get your golden
                                                    string?
That the storm of cruelty affects the faith.
How can you get the comfort of a moon from a silver leaf?
There is no death after this!
If the river stops to flow,
And if the clouds open a way to your heart,
And yes, if the daughter of the moon blesses you with her smiles.
If the mountains become soft, greenery grows
Fruit grows.
And one was kind, from all the unkind.
Will the sun rise?
Will the memories rise with it too?
Those memories that are hidden from our eyes
And while frightened from the flood and the rain of cruelty
Will the light of hope appear?

Nadia Anjuman
Translated from the Dari by Khizra Aslam

Afghan poet **Nadia Anjuman** (1980-2005) published just one volume of poetry *Gul-E-Doudi* (*Black Flower*) in her lifetime. She died as a result of domestic violence; it is said that her husband's family were outraged that she had written about love and beauty. One of her poems contains the prophetic line: 'My words of love speak of death'.

'Nazm' is the poetic form of this poem; Anjuman generally didn't title her poems.

A Women's Issue

The woman in the spiked device
that locks around the waist and between
the legs, with holes in it like a tea strainer
is Exhibit A.

The woman in black with a net window
to see through and a four-inch
wooden peg jammed up
between her legs so she can't be raped
is Exhibit B.

Exhibit C is the young girl
dragged into the bush by the midwives
and made to sing while they scrape the flesh
from between her legs, then tie her thighs
till she scabs over and is called healed.
Now she can be married.
For each childbirth they'll cut her
open, then sew her up.
Men like tight women.
The ones that die are carefully buried.

The next exhibit lies flat on her back
while eighty men a night
move through her, ten an hour.
She looks at the ceiling, listens
to the door open and close.
A bell keeps ringing.
Nobody knows how she got there.

You'll notice that what they have in common
is between the legs. Is this

why wars are fought?
Enemy territory, no man's
land, to be entered furtively,
fenced, owned but never surely,
scene of these desperate forays
at midnight, captures
and sticky murders, doctors' rubber gloves
greasy with blood, flesh made inert, the surge
of your own uneasy power.

This is no museum.
Who invented the word *love*?

Margaret Atwood

Margaret Atwood (born 1939) is probably Canada's best-known novelist and
has been nominated for the Booker Prize five times, winning it once for *The
Blind Assassin* (2000). *Surfacing* (1972) is a feminist classic, blending ecological
concerns into the narrative in a manner prescient of fiction to come. She is also
an accomplished poet and critic, and her work demonstrates an engagement with
ideas with a social resonance and the question of power in our world.

Dear Fahimeh

That day,
that hot day in July,
when the Evin loudspeakers
called out your beautiful name and your lips
smiled, your eyes said to your friends,
'So today is the day.'

You went and your walk
was a perfume filling the corridor.
Everyone gasped, everyone asked with their eyes,
'Is today then the day?' The Pasdar
flung back an answer: 'Where is her bag?
Where are her veil, her socks, her money?'

A rumour went round that you'd given a sign
that yes, today was the day:
'I don't need my food,' you had said.

So tonight is the night.
A silence hangs in the heart of it.
Friends look at friends and tell themselves
that perhaps you'll come back.

Fahimeh dear, tell us, spare
a word for your friends. Is
the sky sad where you are, does it weep?
And the wind, does it ruffle your veil?
Back there, the ward sweats for your news.

And a message gets through:
wind-blown breathless dandelion
comes from the mountains to say that clouds

are massing up there and they're big with child.

Head held high, you are standing and waiting for this,
for the clouds to open, for you
to be mother of change.

Rifles crack.
The moorland holds its breath
at a star shooting across it.

It would be good to sing and go with friends
to face the firing squad, to dance,
to float in the rain.

In the long sea-silence,
a wave lifts, oars clip at the water.

A young fisherman bringing his boat to land,
rice-growers trudging home,
they shape their lips to your name.

Your name is beautiful for young girls born in July.

Author unknown
Translated from the Farsi by Hubert Moore and Nasrin Parvaz

This poem is for Fahimeh Taghadosi, executed in Iran in 1982. It was
memorized by another prisoner Farkhondeh Ashena and then brought to the
wider world's attention when she escaped from Iran.
　　Evin prison is located in northwestern Tehran and is known for its political
prisoners' wing. Photography of the prison complex is strictly forbidden.
　　A 'Pasdar' is a warder.

Rich Woman, Poor Woman

I am a woman.
I am a woman.

I am a woman born of a woman whose man owned a factory.
I am a woman born of a woman whose man laboured in a factory.

I am a woman whose man wore silk suits, who constantly watched his weight.
I am a woman whose man wore tattered clothing, whose heart was constantly strangled by hunger.

I am a woman who watched two babies grow into beautiful children.
I am a woman who watched two babies die because there was no milk.

I am a woman who watched twins grow into popular college students with summers abroad.
I am a woman who watched three children grow, but with bellies stretched from no food.

But then there was a man;
But then there was a man;

And he talked about peasants getting richer by my family getting poorer.
And he told me of days that would be better, and he made the days better.

We had to eat rice.
We had rice.

We had to eat beans!
We had beans.

My children were no longer given summer visas to Europe.
My children no longer cried themselves to sleep.

And I felt like a peasant.
And I felt like a woman.

A peasant with a dull, hard, unexciting life.
Like a woman with a life that sometimes allowed a song.

And I saw a man.
And I saw a man.

And together we began to plot with the hope of the return to freedom.
I saw his heart begin to beat with the hope of freedom, at last.

Someday, the return to freedom.
Someday freedom.

And then,
But then,

One day,
One day,

There were planes overhead and guns firing close by.
There were planes overhead and guns firing in the distance.

I gathered my children and went home.
I gathered my children and ran.

And the guns moved farther and farther away.
But the guns moved closer and closer.

And then, they announced that freedom had been restored!
And then they came, young boys really.

They came into my home along with my man.
They came and found my man.

Those men whose money was almost gone –
They found all of the men whose lives were almost their own.

And we all had drinks to celebrate.
And they shot them all.

The most wonderful martinis.
They shot my man.

And they asked us to dance.
And they came for me.

Me.
For me, the woman.

And my sisters.
For my sister.

And then they took us,
Then they took us,

They took us to dinner at a small, private club.
They stripped from us the dignity we had gained.

And they treated us to beef.
And then they raped us.

It was one course after another.
One after another they came after us.

We nearly burst we were so full.
Lunging, plunging – sisters bleeding, sisters dying.

It was magnificent to be free again!
It was hardly a relief to have survived.

The beans have almost disappeared now.
The beans have disappeared.

The rice – I've replaced it with chicken or steak.
The rice, I cannot find it.

And the parties continue night after night to make up for the time wasted.
And my silent tears are joined once more by the midnight cries of my children,

And I feel like a woman again.
They say, I am a woman.

Author and translator unknown

This reflection was written by a working-class Chilean woman in 1973, shortly after Chile's socialist president, Salvador Allende, was overthrown. A US missionary translated the work and brought it with her when she was forced to leave Chile.

The CIA-backed coup d'état that overthrew the Allende administration and brought General Augusto Pinochet's military regime into power in 1973 was characterized by widespread repression. People perceived as political enemies simply 'disappeared'– hundreds of thousands were incarcerated and tortured, and at least 3,200 killed. Rape was widely used as an instrument of torture.

Every Day

War is no longer declared,
but rather continued. The outrageous
has become the everyday. The hero
is absent from the battle. The weak
are moved into the firing zone.
The uniform of the day is patience,
the order of merit is the wretched star
of hope over the heart.

It is awarded
when nothing more happens,
when the bombardment is silenced,
when the enemy has become invisible
and the shadow of eternal weapons
covers the sky.

It is awarded
for deserting the flag,
for bravery before a friend,
for the betrayal of shameful secrets
and the disregard
of every command.

Ingeborg Bachmann
Translated from the German by Peter Filkins

Ingeborg Bachmann (1926-1973) was an Austrian poet and author, who
started out as a script writer and editor for a radio station. She had a doctorate
in philosophy and was greatly concerned in her writings with the problem of
establishing the truth.

War Triptych: Silence, Glory, Love

I. Accounting

The mother asked to stay.
She looked at her silent child.

I was waiting for you.

The quiet of the girl's face was a different quiet.
Her hands lay untouched by death.

The washer of bodies cut
away her long black dress.

Blue prayer beads fell
to the floor in a slow accounting.

The washer of bodies began to sing
a prayer to mothers and daughters.

The mother said,
who will wait for me.

II. Father Receives News His Son Died in the Intifada

When he heard the news, Mr Karim became silent.
He did not look at the cameras,
nor at the people who brought their grief.
He felt a hand slip from his hand,
a small unclasping,
and for that he refused the solace of glory.

III. Always for the First Time

We tell our stories of war like stories
of love, innocent as eggs.

But we will meet memory again
at the wall around our city,

always for the first time.

Gabeba Baderoon

Gabeba Baderoon (born 1969) is a South African poet with three collections
to her credit. The poem above is the concluding poem of *The Dream in the Next
Body* (2005).

In a radio interview, Baderoon says: 'Its three parts have been inspired by
reports of violence in Iraq and in Palestine, and the concluding section speaks a
little bit more about the situation of human beings as a whole. I wrote that poem
in the aftermath of 2003 when the world saw the invasion of Iraq and images of
the vast tragedies of people who were in a situation of war which they had not
asked for. During that time some people's losses seemed to mean less than others'
and that terrible anonymity struck me so deeply as a kind of moral challenge: not
to accept the idea that somebody else's loss is worth less than mine.'

Nigger Sweat

*'Please have your passport and all documents out and ready for
your interview. Kindly keep them dry.'*
*(Notice in the waiting-room of the US Embassy, Visa Section,
Kingston, Jamaica, 1982.)*

No disrespect, mi boss,
just honest nigger sweat;
well almost, for is true
some of we trying to fool you
so we can lose weself
on the Big R ranch
to find a little life,
but, boss, is hard times
make it, and not because
black people born wutliss:
so, boss, excuse this nigger sweat.
And I know that you know it
as good as me,
this river running through history,
this historical fact, this sweat
that put the aroma
in your choice Virginia
that sweeten the cane
and make the cotton shine:
and sometimes I dream a nightmare dream
that the river rising, rising
and swelling the sea and I see
you choking and drowning
in a sea of black man sweat
and I wake up shaking
with shame and remorse
for my mother did teach me,
Child, don't study revenge.

Don't think we not grateful, boss
how you cool down the place for we comfort,
but the line shuffle forward
one step at a time
like Big Fraid hold we,
and the cool-cut, crew-cut Marine boy
wid him ice-blue eye and him walkie-talkie
dissa walk through the place and pretend
him no see we.
But a bring me handkerchief,
mi mother did bring me up right,
and, God willing, I keeping things cool
till we meet face to face,
and a promise you, boss,
if I get through I gone,
gone from this bruk-spirit, kiss-me-arse place.

Edward Baugh

Edward Baugh (born 1936, Port Antonio, Jamaica) has had a distinguished academic career and is the foremost authority on the West Indian Nobel laureate Derek Walcott.

   The phrase 'nigger sweat' harks back to the US's history of slavery, but also has a prominent place in the William Faulkner short story of Southern decay 'Barn burning'.

   'Big Fraid' is a spook from an Afro-American folktale of the South.

Trench Town Shock (A Soh Dem Sey)

Waia, Miss May, trouble dey yah,
Ban yuh belly, Missis, do.
Mi ha' one terrible piece o' news,
An mi sarry fe sey it consarn yuh.

Yuh know yuh secon' or t'ird cousin?
Yuh great-aunt Edith Fred?
Im pick up imse'f gawn a pickcha show,
An police shot im dead.

But a di bwoy own fault yah mah,
For im go out o' im way
Fi gawn fas' wid police-man,
At leas' a soh dem sey.

Dem sey im a creep oba di teata fence,
Dem halla 'who go deh?'
De bwoy dis chap one bad wud mah,
At leas' a soh dem sey.

Still, nutten woulda come from i',
But what yuh tink, Miss May?
Di bwoy no pull out lang knife mah!
At leas' a soh dem sey.

Dem try fi aim afta im foot
But im head get een di way,
Di bullit go 'traight through im brain,
At leas' a soh dem sey.

Dry yuh yeye, mah, mi know i hat,
But i happen ebery day,
Knife-man always attack armed police
At leas' a soh dem sey.

Valerie Bloom

Valerie Bloom (born 1956), poet and novelist, grew up in Clarendon, Jamaica. Moving to England in 1979, Caribbean life and culture continue to influence much of her writing. Bloom is a spirited performer of her own poetry, which has been widely anthologized.

In this poem, the surface irony and unintentional humour of the speaker's voice in reporting the 'official version' of events (the recurrent refrain of 'at least, that's what they say'), contains within it a tragic tale of police violence. The effect on the recipient of the news is in no doubt (as evidenced by the speaker's injunction to her: 'Dry your eyes, I know it hurts').

The Jamaican Constabulary Force has a well-earned reputation for being corrupt and trigger-happy (the record for police killings was 354 people in 1984). Such excesses are committed with total impunity. The Independent Jamaica Council for Human Rights receives an average of one complaint every day about the abuse of police powers.

A Boy against the Wall

Leaning against the wall
near the blackened brick-oven,
the boy waves a blueberry branch
lazily before his face,
and buries his eyes
in its leaves, too ashamed
to tolerate their stares,
that crowd of neighbours
hovering over the walls
like a bunch of crows,
policemen's badges flashing
in the sun, and his father,
still in his pyjamas,
in the middle of the yard,
whipped like a slave.

Sargon Boulus

Sargon Boulus (1944-2007) was an Iraqi Assyrian poet, translator and short-story writer. He is responsible for introducing many Beat and Modernist poets to the Arab world in his translations. He emigrated to the US in the late 1960s where he became part of the Beat generation. His work illustrated his rejection of the ornamentation of much Arabic poetry.

Prayer in the National Stadium

1 November 1973, Santiago, Chile

I pray to you, St Quixote,
visit me today
and in this dreadful night of fear
comfort my delirium,
give me strength to stand
this long night and those to come
even longer and darker
in their cruel hands.

St Sancho,
as this twilight turns to grey,
come and give us bread,
the true sure tenderness
that is in my blood,
the one thing necessary,
for ever and ever.
Amen.

María Eugenia Bravo Calderara
Translated from the Spanish by Dinah Livingstone

María Eugenia Bravo Calderara was a university teacher in Chile at the time of the 1973 coup that overthrew President Allende and established General Augusto Pinochet at the helm. She was imprisoned and tortured in the notorious National Stadium, the largest in the country, which between September and November operated as a concentration camp. Thousands of suspected Allende sympathizers were held and interrogated here, and scores shot in extra-judicial executions. When the junta was finally removed from power, they managed to secure an amnesty for the people involved in such barbarity. Bravo Calderara escaped to exile in England.

Deathfugue

Black milk of daybreak we drink it at evening
we drink it at midday and morning we drink it at night
we drink and we drink
we shovel a grave in the air where you won't lie too cramped
A man lives in the house he plays with his vipers he writes
he writes when it grows dark to Deutschland your golden hair
                                                    Margareta
he writes it and steps out of doors and the stars are all sparkling
                              he whistles his hounds to stay close
he whistles his Jews into rows has them shovel a grave in the
                                                    ground
he commands us play up for the dance

Black milk of daybreak we drink you at night
we drink you at morning and midday we drink you at evening
we drink and we drink
A man lives in the house he plays with his vipers he writes
he writes when it grows dark to Deutschland your golden hair
                                                    Margareta
Your ashen hair Shulamith we shovel a grave in the air where
                              you won't lie too cramped

He shouts dig this earth deeper you lot there you others sing up
                                                    and play
he grabs for the rod in his belt he swings it his eyes are so blue
stick your spades deeper you lot there you others play on for the
                                                    dancing

Black milk of daybreak we drink you at night
we drink you at midday and morning we drink you at evening
we drink and we drink
a man lives in the house your goldenes Haar Margareta

your aschenes Haar Shulamith he plays with his vipers

He shouts play death more sweetly this Death is a master from
Deutschland
he shouts scrape your strings darker you'll rise up as smoke to
the sky
you'll then have a grave in the clouds where you won't lie too
cramped

Black milk of daybreak we drink you at night
we drink you at midday Death is a master aus Deutschland
we drink you at evening and morning we drink and we drink
this Death is ein Meister aus Deutschland his eye it is blue
he shoots you with shot made of lead shoots you level and true
a man lives in the house your goldenes Haar Margarete
he looses his hounds on us grants us a grave in the air
he plays with his vipers and daydreams der Tod ist ein Meister
aus Deutschland

dein goldenes Haar Margarete
dein aschenes Haar Sulamith

Paul Celan
Translated from the German by John Felstiner

Paul Celan (Paul Antschel, 1920-1970) was born into a German-speaking Jewish family in a part of Bukovina, Romania, which is now in the Ukraine. During World War Two, Romania forced large numbers of Jews into ghettoes with eventual deportations to labour camps. Both his parents met their deaths in a labour camp – his father of disease due to the terrible conditions and his mother shot. Celan was haunted by guilt that he hadn't been successful in persuading them to go into hiding. After the war, Celan eventually settled in Paris where he lived until his suicide by drowning in the Seine.

'Todesfugue' ('Deathfugue') is his most famous poem, a complex, incantatory, unsettling vision of the death camps. In this translation, John Felstiner slowly introduces German words and phrases into the English language repetitions, providing some sense of Celan's conflicted relationship with the language. Celan would declare: 'There is nothing on earth that can prevent a poet from writing, not even the fact that he's Jewish and German is the language of his poems.' In his later poems, his use of the language becomes increasingly cryptic and marked by freshly coined words, as though he were inventing it anew.

Despite the nightmarish quality of the poem, the forced dancing and singing were details based in reality. The SS organized such activities among the inmates of extermination camps.

The blue-eyed Nazi commander of the poem is an embodiment of the ideas of race purity which led the Nazis to mass murder on such an unprecedented scale.

The juxtaposition of the German Margarete with the golden hair (another racial signifier) and the Jewish ashen-haired Shulamith (a princess in the Old Testament whose name carries echoes of 'shalom', the Hebrew word for peace) gains a painful intensity by the time the poem closes. The detail of the hair loses all romance and grim connotations well up of the uses of human body parts by the Nazis.

They Are Picked

They are picked
maimed by mines
crossing borders
from troubled nations.
They are picked across the border
murdered in the streets
where they are squatters.
They are picked
at boundaries
picked by flooded rivers
attempting to swim
across borders.
They are picked
by crocodiles
crossing borders
that are rivers.
They are picked
across the border
picking their lives
in trash bins
picking comfort
in drain pipes.
They are picked
in foreign lands
picketing host politicians
who cannot
accommodate them anymore.

Julius Chingono

Zimbabwean poet **Julius Chingono** (born 1946) has worked for most of his life
in the mines as a blaster. His only novel, *Chipo Changu*, was published in 1978
and a collection of poetry and short stories, *Not Another Day*, in 2006.

The Golf Links

The golf links lie so near the mill
That almost every day
The laboring children can look out
And see the men at play.

Sarah N Cleghorn

Sarah Norcliffe Cleghorn (1876-1959) was a Vermont poet, short story
writer and novelist known for her passionate involvement in a variety of
causes – pacifism, animal rights, women's suffrage, prison reform, anti-racism,
opposition to the death penalty and child labour. A Christian socialist, she
referred to her poems on issues of injustice as her 'burning poems'.

Robert Frost, who was a friend, called her 'the complete abolitionist. She has
it in for race prejudice and many other ignobleness besides. Some time I intend
to ask her if she isn't bent on having the world perfect at last.'

Today she is best remembered for the wistful irony of the quatrain printed above
which actually comes out of a larger work – 'Through the Needle's Eye' (1916).

Free at Night

To take off the bra at night
when the day is over
and with it the duty of rigid breasts.
To take off the bra at night
to remove the shell
the constrictor
someone else's skin.
To free oneself from wires
elastic bands fasteners
to cut with scissors the wonderbra.

Every night women return
from the crusade
and free their holy skin.
The straps slide down their shoulders
the hands meet on their back
freeing the ties
and in the solitude of the bedroom
their breasts
like ships
set sail.

Marina Colasanti
Translated from the Portuguese by Luciana Namorato

Brazilian writer **Marina Colasanti** was born in Asmara, Ethiopia, in 1937 to
Italian parents. Her family moved to Rio de Janeiro when Colasanti was 11.
She has worked as a journalist and has over 30 books (both fiction and poetry)
to her credit.

Because the Dawn Breaks

We speak
because when the rain falls
in the mountains
the river slowly swells

Comes rushing down
over boulders
across roads
crumbling bridges
that would hold their power
against its force

We speak
for the same reason
that
the thunder frightens the child
that
the lightning startles the tree

We do not speak
to defy your tenets
though we do
or upset your plans
even though we do
or to tumble
your towers of babel
we speak in spite of the fact
that we do

We speak
because
your plan

is not our plan
our plan
we speak because we dream
because our dreams
are not of living in pig pens
in any other body's
backyard
not of
catching crumbs from tables
not of crawling forever
along the everlasting ant-line
to veer away in quick detour
when the elephant's foot
crashes down
not of having to turn back
when the smell of death
assails our senses
not of striving forever
to catch the image of your Gods
within our creation

We speak
for the same reason
that
the flowers bloom
that the sun sets
that the fruit ripens

because temples built
to honour myths
must crumble
as the dawn breaks
there is nothing you can do
about your feeble bridges
when the rain falls

in the mountains
and swells the flow of rivers

We speak
not to agitate you
but in spite of your agitation
because
we are workers
peasants
leaders
you see
and were not born
to be your vassals

Merle Collins

Merle Collins (born 1950) grew up in Grenada and first pursued an academic career, followed by a stint in the island nation's Ministry of Foreign Affairs. In 1983, the year of the US-led invasion of the country, following a military-assisted revolutionary coup, Collins left Grenada for Britain.

At the time of the publication of her first volume of poetry, *Because the Dawn Breaks* (1985), she was a member of African Dawn, a performing arts group which combined poetry, mime and African music. She has since published two novels, a collection of short stories and another poetry book, *Rotten Pomerack* (1992).

She is Professor of Comparative Literature and English at the University of Maryland in the US.

For Children, A Letter

Dear children, we were of no use to you. You wanted that we
spend our precious
time in your play. You wanted that we, in our play,
include you. You wanted that we become innocent like you.

Dear children, we only told you that life is a battleground where
we fight endlessly. It was we who sharpened our arms. We
only prompted war. It was our anger and hatred that made us
blind. Dear
children, we lied to you.

This is a long night – like a tunnel. From here we can see
outside, and its unclear view. We can see killing and lamentation.
Children, we sent you there. Forgive us. We lied to you
by saying life is a battleground.

Dear children, life is a festival where you are spread out like
laughter.
Life is a green tree upon which you are perched as fluttering
birds.

As some poets have said, life is a tossed-up ball, and
you are, surrounding it, a gathered group of restless feet.

Dear children, if this is not so, it ought to be so.

Mangalesh Dabral
Translated from the Hindi by Sudeep Sen

Mangalesh Dabral (born 1948) is an Indian poet, translator and journalist who
lives in Delhi. He has five published collections of poetry and three of his prose
writings. Growing up in a rural setting in the foothills of the Himalayas, he has
maintained an unassuming quality to his voice, which asks critical questions
about the nature of human existence with a disarming freshness and directness.

Gujarat 2002

There's blood on the streets, so many dying and the dead,
that dark-grained newspapers squint with red.

Fire and skin turn into one blinding sheet, and in any weather
life and charred skin will peel together.

Boards are warped, the steel blackened. Inside
there's a mother in travail, there could be a bride.

Killer and killed are one – they speak the same language.
The vocabulary of guilt has a circumference and a centre.

Gasoline alights with a splash everywhere.
Knives hiss with the same silence where they enter.

Gujarat is not just the corruption of an absolute.
It has manufactured its own corrupt absolutes:

'If night fell on Godhra, we are within our rights
to unload night on innocence elsewhere.'

There is no place here for the lyre and the lute.
In such times is lockjaw the best – to be dumb, to be mute?

Keki N Daruwalla

Keki N Daruwalla (1937) is in the front ranks of Indian poets writing in
English and has published nine volumes of poetry.
    The violence evoked in this poem refers to the mass killings of Muslims
in India's Gujarat state, with the collusion of the authorities. The trigger had
been an attack at Godhra railway station on Hindu zealots who were returning
from a demonstration to build a temple where a mosque had been torn down in
Ayodhya some years ago. The ensuing massacre was a grim confirmation of the
consequences of the religion-based hate politics increasingly being used in India to
sway public sentiment.

The Earth Is Closing On Us

The earth is closing on us, pushing us through the last passage,
             and we tear off our limbs to pass through.
The earth is squeezing us. I wish we were its wheat so we could
             die and live again. I wish the earth was our mother
So she'd be kind to us. I wish we were pictures on the rocks for
             our dreams to carry
As mirrors. We saw the faces of those to be killed by the last of
             us in the last defence of the soul.
We cried over their children's feast. We saw the faces of those
             who'll throw our children
Out of the windows of this last space. Our star will hang up
             mirrors.
Where should we go after the last frontier? Where should the
             birds fly after the last sky?
Where should the plants sleep after the last breath of air? We
             will write our names with scarlet steam.
We will cut off the hand of the song to be finished by our flesh.
We will die here, here in the last passage. Here and here our
             blood will plant its olive tree.

Mahmud Darwish

Translated from the Arabic by Abdullah al-Udhari

Mahmud Darwish (1941-2008) was regarded as the Palestinian National Poet and published over 30 volumes of poetry in his lifetime. Despite his opposition to Israeli policies which had led to much hardship in his early years, he believed that peace was possible and Israel would not be weakened by it.

The Right Word

Outside the door,
lurking in the shadows,
is a terrorist.

Is that the wrong description?
Outside that door,
taking shelter in the shadows,
is a freedom-fighter.

I haven't got this right.
Outside, waiting in the shadows,
is a hostile militant.

Are words no more
than waving, wavering flags?
Outside your door,
watchful in the shadows,
is a guerilla warrior.

God help me.
Outside, defying every shadow,
stands a martyr.
I saw his face.

No words can help me now.
Just outside the door,
lost in shadows,
is a child who looks like mine.

One word for you.
Outside my door,
his hand too steady,

his eyes too hard
is a boy who looks like your son, too.

I open the door.
Come in, I say.
Come in and eat with us.

The child steps in
and carefully, at my door,
takes off his shoes.

Imtiaz Dharker

Imtiaz Dharker (born 1954) is a poet, artist and documentary film-maker. She was born in Lahore to Pakistani parents but grew up in Glasgow, Scotland. She currently divides her time between Mumbai, London and Wales. Her books are usually illustrated with her exquisite line drawings.

For My Torturer, Lieutenant D...

You slapped me –
     no one had ever slapped me –
Electric shock
And then your fist
And your filthy language
I bled too much to be able to blush
All night long
A locomotive in my belly
Rainbows before my eyes
It was as if I were eating my mouth
Drowning my eyes
I had hands all over me
And felt like smiling.

Then one morning a different soldier came
You were as alike as two drops of blood.
Your wife, Lieutenant –
Did she stir the sugar in your coffee?
Did your mother dare to tell you you looked well?
Did you run your fingers through your kids' hair?

Leila Djabali
Translated from the French by Anita Barrows

Leila Djabali (born 1933) was one of many young Algerian intellectuals who were imprisoned for their part in the liberation movement against French colonial rule. This poem was written in the Barberousse Prison in Algiers in 1957.

Small

Yes, we are small
the smallest pebble
in a field of stones.
But have you felt the hurtle
of pebbles pitched
from a mountaintop?

Small,
as the smallest mountain stream
storing rapids, currents,
unknown to wide and lazy valley rivers.

Small,
like the bullet in the bore
of the rifle;
small as the corn waiting to sprout.

Small
as the pinch of salt
that seasons the table.

Small, yes,
you have compressed us, world,
into a diamond.

Small,
you have dispersed us,
scattered us like stars.
We are everywhere in your vision.

Small,
but our borders stretch

from Piuragan telescopes to the moon,
from Lousavan back to Urartu.

Small as the grain of marvellous Uranium which
cannot be broken down, put out or consumed.

Gevorg Emin
Translated from Armenian by Diana Der-Hovanessian

Gevorg Emin (1919-1998), who trained as a hydraulic engineer, was a widely translated and celebrated Armenian poet, and the author of over 30 books of poetry and prose.

Vendor and Child

Is that a shower of gold seeping
through gaps in the thatching of the sky?
What carefully wafting flakes are these
of light on fire, fading, to die

before they touch the woman and child
encamped beneath a municipal
cassia, now leafless, almost stripped
of life-transfusing bark? And when will

we halt beside her meagre tuckshop:
an upturned Lobels biscuit carton:
and buy a cigarette, a handful
of peanuts, and a blighted onion?

She cleared a space opposite the NO
STOPPING sign on Cecil Avenue,
a space she shares with sparrow weavers
bickering, and Matabele ants

that sting, and stink of formic acid,
with mandibles that nip the tendons
of her battered feet, and bear away,
piece by piece, the crumbs of her domain.

Sick, her child is the colour of ash,
a rag doll of hopelessness, symbol
of the new Zimbabwe. Who will buy
a soft tomato from me? Who will

deliver me from a government
of patronage, of cronyism;

a government of the obese, by
the obese, for the obese? Wallets

of flesh on the backs of their necks, folds
of fat behind their knees; like jumping
castles their bums, like teeming purses
their scrota. O who will deliver

us from these who have been coaxed into
temptation? And who will let that slow
light linger, those wafting flakes of fire,
and set the mother and her child aglow?

John Eppel

John Eppel (born 1947) lives in Bulawayo, Zimbabwe, where he teaches
English at Christian Brothers College. He is an acclaimed novelist and poet.

We are Struggling to Understand

We are the middle children of history,
He said

Ours is that dislocation between

spirit and identity
faith and question
integrity and fascination

We are the middle children of history,
He said

Ours is the time of romantic

Solar powered watches
Paperless documents
Controlled births
Political hungers
And negotiated hate, for

We are the middle children of history,
He said

Ours is that moment of

Anthems without nations
Sciences without compassion
Freedoms without expression, again

We are the middle children of history,
He said

Ours is that aspect of modernity
That historical moment

Of interminable self-deception, since

We are the middle children of history,
He said

And we are struggling to understand

Azad Essa

Azad Essa (born 1982) grew up in the dying years of the South African apartheid regime and is a journalist and lecturer (he calls himself an 'accidental academic').

But then again, what's the difference

...But then again, what's the difference
If it rains or it snows?
If murder is supplied retail
Or wholesale – as in war.

Our sacristies are desecrated,
Atop the pulpit
The Enemy sermonizes.
        While we dream
During workdays of holidays and during festivities of sleep.

Rostislav Evdokimov-Vohac
Translated from the Russian by Emily D Johnson

Rostislav Evdokimov-Vohac (born 1950) was expelled from Leningrad State University in 1971, following the arrest of his father on political charges. In 1982 he was arrested for anti-Soviet agitation and propaganda and sentenced to five years in political isolation camps. His first book-length collection of poetry was published by the émigré publishing house Posev in 1986, a year before his release. Evdomikov-Vohac returned to the University and completed his degree, specializing in ancient Greek history. He writes fiction as well as poetry.

Forugh Farrokhzad (1935-1967) was a poet, critic and filmmaker. Her first collection of verse *Asir* (*Captive*, 1955) was also the first in the history of Persian literature to have a recognizably female voice from start to finish.

Married at just 17, she had to relinquish her only child to her husband's family when the marriage ended two years later. Farrokhzad attracted much criticism just for being a divorcee poet in Iran, but her themes of women's choice and the conventions imposed upon them also drew fire. However, she chose to live by her own rules as far as possible, having several relationships with men after her divorce, culminating in one with Ebrahim Golestan, a controversial filmmaker and writer, which is commemorated in the poem opposite.

Her short life ended as a result of a car crash. She remains the most famous woman in Persian-Iranian literature.

The Sin

I sinned, a sin all filled with pleasure
wrapped in an embrace, warm and fiery
I sinned in a pair of arms
that were vibrant, virile, violent.

In that dim and quiet place of seclusion
I looked into his eyes brimming with mystery
my heart throbbed in my chest all too excited
by the desire glowing in his eyes.

In that dim and quiet place of seclusion
as I sat next to him all scattered inside
his lips poured lust on my lips
and I left behind the sorrows of my heart.

I whispered in his ear these words of love:
'I want you, mate of my soul
I want you, life-giving embrace
I want you, lover gone mad'

Desire surged in his eyes
red wine swirled in the cup
my body surfed all over his
in the softness of the downy bed.

I sinned, a sin all filled with pleasure
next to a body now limp and languid
I know not what I did, God
in that dim and quiet place of seclusion.

Forugh Farrokhzad
Translated from the Persian by Ahmad Karimi-Hakkak

Geography Lesson

When the jet sprang into the sky,
it was clear why the city
had developed the way it had,
seeing it scaled six inches to the mile.
There seemed an inevitability
about what on ground had looked haphazard,
unplanned and without style
when the jet sprang into the sky.

When the jet reached ten thousand feet,
it was clear why the country
had cities where rivers ran
and why the valleys were populated.
The logic of geography –
that land and water attracted man –
was clearly delineated
when the jet reached ten thousand feet.

When the jet rose six miles high,
it was clear that the earth was round
and that it had more sea than land.
But it was difficult to understand
that the men on the earth found
causes to hate each other, to build
walls across cities and to kill.
From that height, it was not clear why.

Zulfikar Ghose

Zulfikar Ghose (born 1935) has published numerous short stories, novels, poetry and literary criticism over a long writing career. Born in Sialkot, now in Pakistan, he has lived in Bombay, London and, since 1969, in the US, where he teaches at the University of Texas at Austin.

Revenge

My personal revenge will be your children's
right to schooling and to flowers.
My personal revenge will be this song
bursting for you with no more fears.

My personal revenge will be to make you see
the goodness in my people's eyes,
implacable in combat always
generous and firm in victory.

My personal revenge will be to greet you
'Good morning!' in streets with no beggars,
when instead of locking you inside
they say, 'Don't look so sad.'
When you, the torturer,
daren't lift your head.
My personal revenge will be to give you
these hands you once ill-treated
with all their tenderness intact.

Luis Enrique Mejía Godoy

Translated from the Spanish by Dinah Livingstone

Nicaraguan singer/songwriter **Luis Enrique Mejía Godoy** (born 1945) wrote this
song, using the words of the Sandinista freedom fighter **Tomás Borge** (born 1930).
People like Borge gave the lie to Washington's propaganda about the Sandinistas
as military despots. Borge underwent seven years of imprisonment and torture at
the hands of the Somoza dictatorship's National Guard; his wife was also tortured,
sexually abused and eventually died at the hands of her tormentors.

After the Sandinista Revolution in 1979, Tomás Borge became Nicaragua's
Justice Minister. The story goes that Borge came face to face with his torturer
and responded by saying: 'For your punishment, I forgive you.'

On a larger scale the Sandinistas' 'revenge' was a vision of an inclusive,
humane society for a country they only briefly governed. In 2006, the Sandinistas
again achieved power in Nicaragua when Daniel Ortega was re-elected president.
However, this time around there are charges of misuse of power and corruption.

From the Garden of the Women
Once Fallen: Thyme

Woman alone, living
in a tenement of enmity.
One room of back-biting
standpipe flowing strife.

Recall one dry Sunday
of no rice and peas no meat
how you boiled a handful
of fresh green thyme

to carry the smell of Sunday
as usual.
Thyme, herb of contraction
rising as steaming incense
of save-face.

When you dwell among enemies
you never make them salt your pot.
You never make them know
your want.

Lorna Goodison

Lorna Goodison was born in Kingston, Jamaica, in 1947, one of nine children. She developed an early love of reading as both her mother and a sister were voracious readers. She has worked as a painter, teacher and government official, and published 11 collections of poems.

Goodison on the genesis of this poem: 'I wrote this poem during the 1970s during Jamaica's "Democratic Socialist" experiment. I once interviewed a woman who lived in a new high-rise housing scheme in Kingston's inner city. She told me that when she did not have money to cook the traditional Jamaican Sunday dinner – rice and peas (which is seasoned with thyme) – she boiled thyme so her neighbours would not know about her lack of money.'

These Current Events

for Adrienne

It is a late twentieth-century cliché that we must turn off
the hypersensitive television to distract our truer desire;
that we must switch off all the lamps and overheads,
open the shade to the natural night
with its artificial lights, dress in silk to undress,
play and play until even the nerve endings in our teeth beg
and we throb forcefully with all the affection
of reproducing ourselves in the act that will not.
In the sweat of it all, despite ideology, we shut out
the current events of the afternoon.

A few miles from my office a boat capsizes,
excretes three hundred men and women
into the frigid undertow towards death
or clean prison clothing and free legal assistance.
They are not *poor* by their own standards
and not all the same – teacher, peasant, entrepreneur –
what they fled was a state of dreaming
to the object of that illusion, as thousands before them,
millions behind. One states he is ambitious.
Another admits he has made a *grave error*.
As their bus glides through Queens will they see
the American destitute housed in cardboard boxes?

I cannot look the man in the eye
who asks for *spare change*.
He smells of urine. His teeth are falling out.
Spare, janus word for extra *and* little.
Surplus for one, dear to another. Dear young man,
there is a collective for you, a union, a regiment,

the biblical multitude of spare people,
the redundant masses of spare labor.

Come exhausted and squalid,
come shitcovered, shitfaced, diseased and immune,
prick and cunt, come third world capitalist,
come Chinese laborer whose forefathers
blew tunnels through mountains,
lay track across the continent,
cut cane, starched the white shirts of the bourgeoisie;
whose uncle of your grandmother
fell unconscious under an avalanche of ice
in the Sierra Nevadas and could not be recovered
until the spring thaw. Come to the land of surplus value

where someone will overdose one night
after twenty hours of bussing tables. The stories
you have not heard or if you did you translated their meaning
as propaganda to keep you poor in a poor country
as opposed to poor in a wealthy country.

I cannot look in the face of the man cursing me out
because I don't want my car window washed.
I cannot look at the man, empty cup, empty pant legs,
who flashes a razor at me on his tongue.
I cannot speak to the girl pregnant with addiction
thanking me *for nothing*. I can
pick the paper up any day of the week
and find so much sorrow it is difficult to believe
there are solutions.

In the summer exhaust of a million air conditioners
I turn to my beloved for psalms, for physical reassurance.
The children snore softly behind the fan's whirl
because we have a place to plug in a fan.

If I turn to him or to you, if I turn to sheafs of paper
in order to turn away from these current events
it is only to revive the heartbeat of commitment.
I know poetry cannot save
but it fuels the gut that is able.

Kimiko Hahn

Kimiko Hahn (born 1955) is an American poet and academic who has also
written texts for film. She has seven published collections and has worked on
imagining an 'Asian American aesthetic' which includes engagement with and
the reinvention of classical Japanese and Chinese forms.

Desta

Daughter, Desta, born in exile,
Come home the first time.
Meet your grandmother
Her family, her neighbours –
Your family, your neighbours,
Your country, our home.
Please eat
These vegetables and meat
And a special treat of wild roots.
Or have I spoiled you?

No, Daddy, I love this.
But we need windows.

Reesom Haile

Translated from the Tigrinya by Charles Cantalupo

Reesom Haile (1946-2003) was born, raised and completed his schooling in
Eritrea; he became a radio and television journalist in Ethiopia. Moving to the
United States, he received a doctorate in Media Ecology. In exile, he lectured
at Western universities and worked for international NGOs, until he returned to
Eritrea in 1994 after the end of his country's war of liberation with Ethiopia.

Two books of his verse have been published in English translation: *We Have
Our Voice* (2000) and *We Invented the Wheel* (2002).

You Get Proud by Practicing

If you are not proud
for who you are, for what you say, for how you look;
if every time you stop
to think of yourself, you do not see yourself glowing
with golden light; do not, therefore, give up on yourself.
You can
get proud.

You do not need
a better body, a purer spirit, or a Ph D
to be proud.
You do not need
a lot of money, a handsome boyfriend, or a nice car.
You do not need
to be able to walk, or see, or hear,
or use big, complicated words,
or do any of the things that you just can't do
to be proud. A caseworker
cannot make you proud,
or a doctor.
You only need
more practice.
You get proud
by practicing.

There are many many ways to get proud.
You can try riding a horse, or skiing on one leg,
or playing guitar,
and do well or not so well,
and be glad you tried

either way.
You can show
something you've made
to someone you respect
and be happy with it no matter
what they say.
You can say
what you think, though you know
other people do not think the same way, and you can
keep saying it, even if they tell you
you are crazy.
You can add your voice
all night to the voices
of a hundred and fifty others
in a circle
around a jailhouse
where your brothers and sisters are being held
for blocking buses with no lift,
or you can be one of the ones
inside the jailhouse,
knowing of the circle outside.
You can speak your love
to a friend
without fear.
You can find someone
who will listen to you
without judging you or doubting you or being
afraid of you
and let you hear yourself perhaps
for the first time.
These are all ways
of getting proud.

None of them
are easy, but all of them
are possible. You can do all of these things,
or just one of them again and again.
You get proud
by practicing.

Power makes you proud, and power
comes in many fine forms
supple and rich as butterfly wings.
It is music
when you practice opening your mouth
and liking what you hear
because it is the sound of your own
true voice.
It is sunlight
when you practice seeing
strength and beauty in everyone
including yourself.
It is dance
when you practice knowing
that what you do
and the way you do it
is the right way for you
and can't be called wrong.
All these hold
more power than weapons or money
or lies.
All these practices bring power, and power
makes you proud.
You get proud
by practicing.

Remember, you weren't the one
who made you ashamed,
but you are the one
who can make you proud.
Just practice,
practice until you get proud, and once you are proud,
keep practicing so you won't forget.
You get proud
by practicing.

Laura Hershey

Laura Hershey (born 1962) is a Colorado-based writer, poet, activist and consultant. Hershey's activism stretches over a wide range of disability rights and social justice issues, and she has made important contributions to the visibility of LGBT people with disabilities.

Calls from the Outside World

Celeste called work to leave a message
for Nathan. 'Tell him Celeste called.
Tell him *something happened*'

And that became a famous phone message
and part of the folklore
finally working its way into a byword at the
shop and it came to designate a
call from anyone's spouse or
companion   Hey Richie, line six –
something

And there was an amused pride in
having invented such a good piece of
workplace slang, so specialized and so secret
and so site-specific

but before long Nate was gone and then
one by one nearly everybody else
so today the slang is just as good as ever
but completely forgotten or unknown
to the present staff

So we see that for slang to survive
we require a body of speakers
initiated in its use
large enough to provide continuity
and with a core of permanence
This must be why the linguists
invented prisons, as language laboratories

so that the whole country can imitate
the speech of young black men but
never actually have to see them, so white
golfers can cry *You the man*
and little blond girls can shout
You go, girl

Robert Hershon

Robert Hershon (born 1936) has written 11 books of poems and is the co-editor of Hanging Loose Press, Brooklyn, New York.

Emancipation Proclamation

Whereas it minds its own business
& lives in its one place so faithfully
& its trunk supports us when we lean against it
& its branches remind us of how we think

Whereas it keeps no bank account but hoards carbon
& does not discriminate between starlings and robins
& provides free housing for insects and squirrels
& lifts its heartwood grave into the air

Whereas it holds our firmament in place
& writes underground gospel with its roots
& whispers us oxygen with its leaves
& may not survive its new climate of ultraviolet

We the people for ourselves & our children
necessarily proclaim this tree
free from commerce & belonging to itself
as long as it & we shall live.

William Heyen

William Heyen (born 1940) is a US poet, editor, literary critic and former All-American soccer player. He has had many published collections and is widely anthologized. One of his major themes has been the intersection of ecological destruction and the economy.

Some People

(for Eoin)

Some people know what it's like,

to be called a cunt in front of their children
to be short for the rent
to be short for the light
to be short for school books
to wait in Community Welfare waiting-rooms full of smoke
to wait two years to have a tooth looked at
to wait another two years to have a tooth out (the same tooth)
to be half strangled by your varicose veins, but you're
198th on the list
to talk into a banana on a jobsearch scheme
to talk into a banana in a jobsearch dream
to be out of work
to be out of money
to be out of fashion
to be out of friends
to be in for the Vincent de Paul man
to be in space for the milk man
(sorry, mammy isn't in today she's gone to Mars for the weekend)
to be in Puerto Rico this week for the blanket man
to be in Puerto Rico next week for the blanket man
to be dead for the coal man
(sorry, mammy passed away in her sleep, overdose of coal
                                                in the teapot)
to be in hospital unconscious for the rent man
(St Judes ward 4th floor)
to be second-hand

to be second-class
to be no class
to be looked down on
to be walked on
to be pissed on
to be shat on

and other people don't.

Rita Ann Higgins

Rita Ann Higgins (born 1955) has lived all her life in Galway, Ireland. One of 13 children, she left school at 14, married at 17, and began writing poetry in her late twenties. Today, with several poetry collections and plays under her belt, her poetry does not shy away from politics and is celebrated for telling it like it is.

To 'talk into a banana' refers to the curved mics people talk into when meeting job centre staff.

The 'Vincent de Paul man' – Society of Saint Vincent de Paul is a Catholic charity that works with 'people who experience poverty and exclusion'.

On Living

I

Living is no laughing matter:
     you must live with great seriousness
          like a squirrel, for example –
I mean without looking for something beyond and above living,
          I mean living must be your whole occupation.
Living is no laughing matter:
     you must take it seriously,
     so much so and to such a degree
   that, for example, your hands tied behind your back,
               your back to the wall,
   or else in a laboratory
     in your white coat and safety glasses,
     you can die for people –
even for people whose faces you've never seen,
even though you know living
     is the most real, the most beautiful thing.
I mean, you must take living so seriously
   that even at seventy, for example, you'll plant olive trees –
   and not for your children, either,
   but because although you fear death you don't believe it,
   because living, I mean, weighs heavier.

II

Let's say you're seriously ill, need surgery –
which is to say we might not get up
          from the white table.
Even though it's impossible not to feel sad
          about going a little too soon,

we'll still laugh at the jokes being told,
we'll look out the window to see it's raining,
or still wait anxiously
          for the latest newscast...
Let's say we're at the front –
          for something worth fighting for, say.
There, in the first offensive, on that very day,
          we might fall on our face, dead.
We'll know this with a curious anger,
          but we'll still worry ourselves to death
          about the outcome of the war, which could last years.
Let's say we're in prison
and close to fifty,
and we have eighteen more years, say,
                    before the iron doors will open.
We'll still live with the outside,
with its people and animals, struggle and wind –
                    I mean with the outside beyond the walls.
I mean, however and wherever we are,
          we must live as if we will never die.

III

This earth will grow cold,
a star among stars
          and one of the smallest,
a gilded mote on blue velvet –
          I mean *this*, our great earth.
This earth will grow cold one day,
not like a block of ice
or a dead cloud even
but like an empty walnut it will roll along

in pitch-black space ...
You must grieve for this right now
– you have to feel this sorrow now –
for the world must be loved this much
                    if you're going to say 'I lived' ...

Nazim Hikmet

Translated from the Turkish by Randy Blasing and Mutlu Konuk

Nazim Hikmet (1901-63) was persecuted by the Turkish State for his 'romantic communist' beliefs in an era of Cold War. He spent much of his adult life in and out of prison. This poem was written 10 years into a 28 year sentence (hence the reference to the 18 remaining years). He was released two years later as part of a general amnesty.

He was always widely loved in Turkey, despite being forced to leave the country – he died in Moscow. His reputation continues to grow posthumously. Hikmet's Turkish citizenship, which had been revoked in 1959, was only restored in 2009.

Crocodiles Under the House

Father traveled to other countries

And when he returned, bundles of dollars
Were his coming-home gift to his pet
Crocodiles that always took shelter
Under the house, for they found it hot.

The crocodiles were in a frenzy,
Trying to be first to get a bite at Father's bundles:
'Here's yours, and here also is yours',
Was how the gift was divided
While mother was forgotten, neglected,
Pitiful, dragging herself on her ass in the corner from an illness
That seems to have no cure.

'There is still something coming,' Father assures us –
Something to fix our crumbling house
And to cure Mother's illness.

Antonio S Joquiño, Jr
Translated from the Tagalog by Leoncio P Deriada

Antonio S Joquiño, Jr (born 1956) edits the literary magazine *Yahum* in the Philippines.
'Crocodiles' for Filipinos, are corrupt government officials and the poem satirizes the frequent foreign trips made by the head of state.

Becoming a Brahmin

Algorithm for converting a Shudra into a Brahmin

Begin.

Step 1: Take a beautiful Shudra girl.
Step 2: Make her marry a Brahmin.
Step 3: Let her give birth to his female child.
Step 4: Let this child marry a Brahmin.
Step 5: Repeat steps 3-4 six times.
Step 6: Display the end product. It is a Brahmin.

End.

Algorithm advocated by Father of the Nation at Tirupur.
Documented by Periyar on 20-09-1947.

Algorithm for converting a pariah into a Brahmin.

Awaiting another Father of the Nation
to produce this algorithm.

Inconvenience caused due to inadvertent delay
is sincerely regretted.

Meena Kandasamy

Meena Kandasamy (born 1984) is a poet, fiction writer and translator who lives and works in Chennai, India. She sees her work as a coming to terms with issues of identity: being a woman, a Tamil (a South Indian in the North-dominated national culture) and of 'low' caste. She has edited a Dalit magazine and is a member of the Dalit Panther movement (the Dalits being the former 'untouchables', at the bottom of the heap in the Hindu caste system).

Shudras are the lowest caste (just above Dalits) and Brahmins the highest.

'Father of the Nation' is a reference to Gandhi, seen by many as a champion of the rights of 'untouchables'. However, critics argue that Gandhi did not go far enough in challenging the issues of continued high caste leadership or indeed in working towards the dismantling of caste altogether. Rather he argued for compassion and change from within the caste structure, a position that Dalit activists would see as not being radical enough.

Periyar E V Ramasamy, a Tamil socio-political reformer, both clashed and co-operated with Gandhi on issues of Brahmin domination and caste. Periyar felt that 'Gandhi adapted Brahmins to social change without depriving them of their leadership'.

Caste continues to be a major factor in human rights abuses in India, despite a rising tide of Dalit activism.

Who Gives the Other One?

So this is what a woman's soul needs: to know
where my place is, who is the master of the house.
My love holds a power-demonstration,
God save the porcelain crockery.

Don't do it – I would whisper gently to him,
but I feel it's better if I'm silent now.
My chief virtue is quick adaptation,
I easily become the ideal subject of suffering.

Behold, here I stand. Neither drama, nor poetry.
My love calls me a frigid cunt,
my solid value-system seems to be crumbling.

(Sweet little pillar of salt – I think of myself,
while I stare at the slammed door.
Behold, here I stand. I lean my head against the wall.)

Orsolya Karafiath

Translated from the Hungarian by David A Hill with Ildikó Juhász

Orsolya Karafiath (born 1976) is a Hungarian poet with two published collections, who has also performed her work on CD with musical backing.

The title of this poem derives from a Hungarian saying 'I'll give you such a big slap that the wall will give you the other one!', implying that the receiver's head will be turned around so much by the force of the slap, that their other cheek will be hit in the same way by the adjacent wall.

from Perfect Circle

What are you doing, my child?
I'm dreaming, Mother, dreaming
I'm singing you're asking me
what are you doing, my son?
What does the song in your dream
say, my child? Mother,
it says that once I had a house
and now we have none, Mother.
That's what it says,
that I once had a voice and a language
and now I have no voice and no language.
With the voice that I lost in the
language I lost
I sing a song, Mother,
about the house that I lost.

Ademir Kenović, Abdulah Sidran

These are lines from *Savršeni Krug* (*Perfect Circle*, 1997), the first Bosnian film to emerge after Bosnia Herzegovina became a sovereign state. Directed by **Ademir Kenović** (born 1950), and scripted by Kenović and **Abdulah Sidran** (born 1944), the film tells of two boys aged nine and seven, who, upon losing their parents in the first year of the war, find a haven in a Sarajevo poet's house.

Kenović stresses that it is not a war film, but that the war is the backdrop to a tale of three people learning to live together and love one another. Writer and poet Sidran is best known for his screenplays, including the Cannes prizewinner *When Father Was Away On Business*.

Sleeping on the Street

Removing your clothes like old newsprint
I lay you down raw on a damp mattress and look down on you.
Your gnarled hands and feet have lost their vigour
How weary the skinny limbs and ribs look.
I'm sorry.
Using you, I earned a living,
got a woman and set up house but
the only things left are stale sweat and a nightmare road.
Again I laid the pure thing you are
in a secluded corner of unfamiliar ground.
Alas!
I'm not saying there were no good days, yet
the way to paying even a meagre wage for your labours is far
away.

Now I'm wondering if I would like to go away quietly,
simply leaving you sleeping here.
What about it, body?

Kim Sa-In
Translated from the Korean by Brother Anthony of Taizé

Kim Sa-In was a 2006 recipient of a Daesan Foundation award, the premier
prize for literature in the Korean language.

Sun Mass

The dark precedes the sun,
the sun destroys the dark.
Reality precedes dreams,
and then dreams destroy reality.
Hey, eagle taking the sun for a stroll
now, behind the wall of clouds,
I dare
to dream
that the sun's mysterious corpuscular waves
are linking my life to the sun.
To prevent my life from becoming an ashtray
to prevent my life from becoming
an icy mask
I dare imagine:
my fire revolving as the sun in its eternal orbit.
For ever, eternally.
Unite
my life and that enormous life.
What spinning wheel
in the void of what fog
is our thread becoming unwoven?

Kim Sŭng-hŭi
Translated from the Korean by Brother Anthony of Taizé

Kim Sŭng-hŭi (born 1952) writes both poetry and fiction. Her books of verse
include *Life in the Egg* (1989).

Impassable Bridge

I phoned for an MP
A former bosom friend.
His secretary asked,
In connection with what?

It punctured my ego,
I felt my manhood shrinking.

I said,
Give him my message
Tell him that poisonous mushrooms
Sprout under rotten logs.
If he asks for my name
Say it was an angered poet.
If you can do that for me
I'll be OK.

But she was quick to add,
She said,
And lizards don't fly
For their food
They crawl.

She hung up.

Mzi Mahola

Mzi Mahola (Mzikayise Winston Mahola, born 1949) began writing poetry while still at school. In 1976 his poetry manuscripts were confiscated by the State Security forces of the then apartheid regime in South Africa, which made him stop writing for the next 13 years. Two books of poetry, *Strange Things* (1994) and *When Rains Come* (2000) have been well received.

The Slipper

One day a few months ago
an old woman appeared
at the entrance of the underground station.
She was begging.

Her clothes were torn but white as white.
She reminded me of my grandmother:
her eyes full of fear,
her last days.

Each time I passed by her
I made a habit of saying 'Good morning,'
and giving her some bread or money.
She never said a word.

The other day I tried to say more,
she looked, but obviously didn't understand.
She took what I gave her,
turned her head the other way.

When I passed by yesterday,
she wasn't at her usual place,
on the ground I saw a single slipper
in faded pink, sequined, on its left side

a blood-red plastic heart.
Tiny and glittering.
As if it would, at any moment
start beating.

Roni Margulies
Translated from the Turkish by Saliha Paker and Mel Kenne

Caligula's Horse

And it came to pass that Caligula's horse
Was proclaimed senator.

A fair horse, almost divine,
It strode majestically into the hall,
Greeted everyone with due regard,
Taking no notice of rank or office, even of the ministers,
And went straight to its appointed place
Modestly,
       As if it were ashamed of being there.

It immediately saw through those around it,
Murderers, profiteers, sycophants, wheelers and dealers
It never assented
       to the conquest of other countries,
To the lowering of salaries, or to the raising of prices,
Nor did it take any notice of pompous speeches,
Never did it applaud,
       but listened to the speeches of the orators
              with sheer indifference
And it never dreamed of taking advantage of its senatorial
Position to publish fat books.

On occasion, glancing at the sleepy faces of its citizens,
It would dream of how it used to frolic in the meadows,
Of the clear blue sky, of spring water.

Later it was engulfed by such sorrow
That the senators began looking askance at it,
They began murmuring about its wild past,

About the dubious company it kept, about its unbridled lifestyle.

Nonetheless, it lived a long life
And it used its power better than anyone else had,
That is:
    not at all!

Rudolf Marku
Translated from the Albanian by Robert Elsie

Rudolf Marku (born 1952) introduced many new and previously ostracized writers to Albanian readers through his editorship of the literary newspaper *Drita* (*The Light*). Marku's first collection, *Shokët e mi* (*My Friends*, 1974), led to his banishment to the countryside. It was followed by four other collections and by 1991 he was appointed head of foreign cultural relations at the Albanian Foreign Ministry.

The Roman emperor Caligula (12-41), whose reign has become a byword for debauchery and misuse of power, doted on his horse Incitatus and wanted to make him a consul.

(*See page 95*) **Roni Margulies** (born 1955) grew up in Istanbul but moved to London in the early 1970s, and now spends his time in both cities.

He has published seven volumes of poetry characterized by a clear and precise speaking voice that articulates a cosmopolitan, urban sensibility. His academic background is in economics and he is a trenchant critic of free-market ideology.

Il Capitano

He keeps a dark shed by the beachhuts and boathouses
smelling of diesel and damp wool;
there's a yellowed notice tacked to the door
in a strange hand or a strange tongue like the babble
of waves on pebbles, cursives of broken shell.

Rigged out in nets and tackle, he carries a trident
to tap the ground in the tireless walking
that keeps him always in sight of the sea
where the spiny rocks sift back the waves
like krill-less drizzle from the teeth of whales.

The villagers tell how once, years back,
he commanded a vessel wrecked miles out
and drifted days on a fragment of deck.
Ever since his rescue he's lived like the last man alive
in this coast resort buzzing with tourists and Vespas.

He was washed up here like the rest of us
by seed, tide, trade or fate but clearly lives,
oblivious of custom, under a different sky
– the stars urgent and legible, the miles of black salt
crushing into coves, his intimate blueprint.

It's said that sometimes he sights a ship
far out in the blue and foams with an exquisite
panic of recognition. Dropping his stick
he thrashes through the waves like a fierce child
till the fishermen gently drag him back again.

Jamie McKendrick

Jamie McKendrick (born 1955) is an award-winning British poet, the author
of six collections of poetry, and an accomplished translator of Italian literature.

Let's fill in the form: date of birth

Let's fill in the form: date of birth –
that's the start of the delusion,
the start of delirium or dream…
The problem is clear, it seems.
And in the box below the date
we give our address and phone number;
on the left – our sex, lower on the right
we give our nationality,
then the signature. Well, is life clearer
now and how to manage it?

Larisa Miller
Translated from the Russian by Richard McKane

Larisa Miller (born 1940) lives in Moscow and has published eight books of prose and poetry.

The ultimate rendition

is
to find a word
of quiet dignity, impeccably
connected (music, literature),
that will ask no questions
and will stop at nothing
(not the sending

of a man
across a sea by plane
to somewhere else so somewhere else
can torture him and we don't have to)

and will make it seem
a mild necessity, it happens,

like the sea's gesticulations,
clenching, heaving upwards
as the plane flies over,

like dread
that trickles coldly down the spine,

like handcuffing-sores, like sobs.

Hubert Moore

Hubert Moore (born 1934) is a British poet with six published poetry
collections, of which the latest is *The Hearing Room* (Shoestring, 2006).

A Memory

They threw the children
from the burning train
out onto the grass.
I slithered and swam
in a bloody trench
of bone, gristle, guts.

The pilot who flew overhead,
this scion of the brownshirt blight,
grinned like an invalid,
finally out of his mind.
He hovered in his airborne cage,
pressed to the cockpit glass.
I saw the swastika on his arm,
the sweat on his brow, the rage.

And I saw, too, the red circle
of the locomotive's wheel.
And fear robbed me
of the strength to exclude
everything I had seen –
because the engine was motionless,
yet the blood-red fumes
rose from the wheels, turning still,
and the iron lever groaned –
it was like an arm, crooked at the elbow,
torn from the trunk it served,
to keep the locomotive's wheels
posthumously going round!

This was in the fifth year of my life.
The Good Lord rescued me

for the long way that lay ahead...
But in my blood, like mercury,
is the dread that entered my flesh!
And now, in the moon's view, as I sleep,
so wildly do I lament
that the very wall where the memory
is stored streams with tears.

Yunna Morits

Translated from the Russian by Daniel Weissbort

Yunna Morits (born 1937) is a poet and visual artist, whose early years were marked by hardship – the imprisonment of her father by Stalin, childhood tuberculosis, World War Two and prejudice against Jews in Russia.

The poem above is based on a memory from childhood when she was being evacuated from Kiev and the train she was in was bombed.

In the 1950s she was expelled from her studies in Moscow because of her alienation from the Soviet system. She is a member of the Human Rights Commission of Russian Section of International PEN.

A Will

To Lamia' the female

To you my little daughter
The ringing of the murmurs
I silenced
The sad laughter
I drowned
The ecstasy of scents
I buried
When my youth wandered away

To you
All the paths
I never trod

All the waves...
I never struggled with
Fear O my dear
Is the sailor's enemy

To you
All the fruit
My hands forbore...
From picking

Fatiha Morchid
Translated by Norddine Zouitni

Fatiha Morchid (born 1958) is a paediatric physician who has also presented medical programmes on Moroccan television. Not having followed the literary academic route to writing poetry, her poems present a direct voice that does not conform to traditional literary norms and is uninterested in obscurity.

The Men Next Door

The ten men next door are going to die
tomorrow. They are singing their last hymn:
'A pilgrim was I wandering...'
in their cell without an outside. At this final
hour, God seems to be where they have been
going all this time. If so, they have arrived.
Their cell, like mine, has three corners. In one,
imitating Lazarus, God is squatting, holding his chin.
He's listening to the most solemn final
wishes. But he is not moved; it is true, I believe now,
that God does leisurely watch his own creations
being destroyed. In another corner, the radiogram
that Reverend Father Charles bought from his own savings
and brought into the cell next door
– so the reports go,
is bleating *skokiaan*. But none of the men is
dancing. I can't see what's in the third corner
now, my eyes have grown so bad during this sojourn
in a condemned cell.
Yesterday the ten men were given huge mutton,
spinach and brown beans, but the food lies on the
floor, putrefying. Today, on the eve of their death,
the ten men were allowed warm baths. They have taken none
of it, vowing that they are not just pigs reared
for their bacon. They sing to beat *skokiaan*.
By my side, Victor Ndovi cannot sleep. Indeed no one
is sleeping in my baggy cell of forty, the size of the cell
occupied by the ten men who are going to die tomorrow.
The windows are shut, but Victor and I have heard
it pour in the condemned cell next door
since its occupants, the ten men who are going to die
tomorrow were admitted there.

To do them homage the whole world is quiet; but
the Kings African Rifles memorial clock
at the square outside still whirs, lest we forget
our own condemnation.
Next week, next month or next year
(for events take their own time in these precincts)
I will be moved next door with nine others.
I shake at how I shall perform; for I'm
dead, already dead
in this.

Zomba Central Prison, August 1973

Edison Mpina

The late **Edison Mpina** was a Malawian poet whose books included *Raw Pieces* (1986), *The Low Road to Death* (1991) and *Freedom Avenue* (1991). He won the BBC Arts and Africa poetry competition in 1981.
skokiaan: Popular music that originated from South Africa which is also a symbol of the gallows.

We are not responsible

We are not responsible for your lost or stolen relatives. We
cannot guarantee your safety if you disobey our instructions.
We do not endorse the causes or claims of people begging for
handouts. We reserve the right to refuse service to anyone. Your
ticket does not guarantee that we will honor your reservations.
In order to facilitate our procedures, please limit your carrying
on. Before taking off, please extinguish all smoldering
resentments. If you cannot understand English, you will be
moved out of the way. In the event of a loss, you'd better look
out for yourself. Your insurance was cancelled because we can
no longer handle your frightful claims. Our handlers lost your
luggage and we are unable to find the key to your legal case.
You were detained for interrogation because you fit the profile.
You are not presumed to be innocent if the police have reason
to suspect you are carrying a concealed wallet. It's not our fault
you were born wearing a gang color. It is not our obligation to
inform you of your rights. Step aside, please, while our officer
inspects your bad attitude. You have no rights that we are bound
to respect. Please remain calm, or we can't be held responsible
for what happens to you.

Harryette Mullen

Harryette Mullen (born 1953) grew up in Texas influenced by many of the
popular movements of the 1960s and 1970s, including Civil Rights, Black Power
and feminism. Her poetry addresses questions of identity politics, globalization
and consumerism, often deploying humour. She is author of six poetry books and
teaches at the University of California at Los Angeles in the US.

Electric Lights Come to Puttalli

Children wake up run a rope round the pulley
of the jasmine well and water laughs
birds preen their wings something flashes
in the field and urchins play *cinni dandu*
near the river

carts silently descend in the distance
cart behind cart behind cart behind cart

as the sun climbs the sky shadows lean
water warms in the river the rays pour
all over bald heads and down down down
come people in carts magical people
wearing blue

bringing poles the whole length of the carts
stretching before and behind
weird calculations at the edge of the brain
scratching at wonder a fear of deep things
at the fingertips

climbing them with eyes speaking silent meanings
the people wearing blue bring down the poles
balance them from street to street multiplying
numbers and leaving bootprints without a toe
snake-hood patterns in the dirt

uncoiling a coil of copper digging pits
planting poles pouring salt pouring water
burying a meaning in a language no one knows there
leaving not a street alley corner or turning
they spread a net of wire

grow long in shadow as the day declines
becoming night with anxiety's nets of wire below
crowds gather as at a fair mouths gaping
standing rooted like rows of poles like the rows
of electric poles

even as they look on the blue ones suddenly
laugh climb up and up on the poles the blue people
become specks and melt away in the blue

H S Venkatesh Murthy
Translated from the Kannada by A K Ramanujan

H S Venkatesh Murthy (born 1944) is a leading Kannada language poet, playwright and translator. He lives in Bangalore, India.
Puttalli: little village
cinni dandu: a game played with a short whittled piece (*cinni*) and a longer stick (*dandu*)

Boycott

(Composed at the beginning of repression in Ottoman times, when the Publication Law was imposed on free thought in the Arab World.)

By sea, by land, harass us:
Scatter our best
And kill our free
One by one.

In the long run
Good will remain good
And evil,
Evil.

Smash our pens!
Will smashing them
Prevent our hands
From carving on the stones?

Cut off our hands!
Will cutting them off
Prevent our eyes
From flashing out our anger?

Put out our eyes!
Will putting them out
Prevent our chests
From heaving deep sighs?

Stop our breathing…!
And that's the limit of your power.

It puts us far beyond your reach.
Thank you.

Khalil Mutran

Translated from the Arabic by Issa Boullata and Thomas G Ezzy

Khalil Mutran (1872-1949) was a Syrian poet who lived most of his life in Egypt, having fled there from Ottoman oppression. He was one of the pioneers of narrative verse in Arabic poetry, using it to voice dissent.

Character

You're a girl
    and you'd better not forget
    that when you cross the threshold of your house
    men will look askance at you.

When you keep on walking down the lane
    men will follow you and whistle.

When you cross the lane and step onto the main road
    men will revile you, call you a loose woman.

    If you've no character
    you'll turn back,
    and if you have
    you'll keep on going
    as you're going now.

Taslima Nasrin

Taslima Nasrin (born 1962) grew up in a highly conservative environment in Bangladesh. A love of literature combined with her study of science, and she started publishing poetry and articles about women's rights alongside her work as a physician. Her freethinking nature won her admirers and enemies in equal measure, and as her publications began to reach an ever-widening audience, threats from fundamentalists became common.

The turning point came in 1993 with the publication of *Lajja* (*Shame*), a documentary novel about the treatment of the minority Hindu community in Bangladesh. Islamist fundamentalists issued a fatwa against her and a price was put on her head. The following year she escaped to Sweden.

Since then Nasrin has suffered much censure and malicious litigation due to the outspoken nature of her writing and has moved from country to country. A stay in West Bengal, India, a place with cultural similarities to her homeland, including a common language, was recently curtailed due to pressure from fundamentalists. She is currently living in the United States.

Irregular Verbs

These are some verbs that, at a snail's pace,
I conjugate
You conjugate
He conjugates
As without constitutional guarantees all become inhibited
I don't write
You don't write
He doesn't write
For to write the things that one holds in one's head
I am arrested
You are arrested
He is arrested

Aquiles Nazoa
Translated from the Spanish by Vanessa Baird

Aquiles Nazoa (1920-76) began a journalistic career after first starting work on the Venezuelan newspaper *El Universal* as a packer. He graduated to proofreading and then on to journalism. His wit and humour were widely admired. He was once arrested and even expelled from the country for a brief period for his writing. He was committed to universal education and human rights – two of the themes also of this short poem.

The United Fruit Co.

When the trumpet sounded, it was
all prepared on the earth,
and Jehovah parcelled out the earth
to Coca Cola, Inc., Anaconda,
Ford Motors, and other entities:
The Fruit Company, Inc.
reserved for itself the most succulent,
the central coast of my own land,
the delicate waist of America.
It rechristened its territories
as the 'Banana Republics'
and over the sleeping dead,
over the restless heroes
who brought about the greatness,
the liberty and the flags,
it established the comic opera:
abolished the independencies,
presented crowns of Caesar,
unsheathed envy, attracted
the dictatorship of the flies,
Trujillo flies, Tacho flies,
Carias flies, Martines flies,
Ubico flies, damp flies
of modest blood and marmalade,
drunken flies who zoom
over the ordinary graves,
circus flies, wise flies
well trained in tyranny.

Among the blood-thirsty flies
the Fruit Company lands its ships,
taking off the coffee and the fruit;

the treasure of our submerged
territories flow as though
on plates into the ships.

Meanwhile Indians are falling
into the sugared chasms
of the harbours, wrapped
for burial in the mist of the dawn:
a body rolls, a thing
that has no name, a fallen cipher,
a cluster of dead fruit
thrown down on the dump.

Pablo Neruda

Translated from the Spanish by Robert Bly

Pablo Neruda (1904-73) was Chile's most celebrated poet of recent times and
a winner of the Nobel Prize for Literature in 1971. He was a friend of Salvador
Allende, who appointed him Chile's Ambassador to France, and died soon after
the coup that replaced Allende with a military dictatorship.

The United Fruit Company was a US corporation which owned gigantic
plantations (of mainly bananas and pineapples) in Latin America and the West
Indies. The Company's struggle for monopoly was to affect the political course
of many Latin American countries, a form of exploitative economic neo-
colonialism which encouraged corruption and authoritarianism, and sought to
eliminate workers rights.

Trujillo, Tacho, Carias, Martines and Ubico: South American dictators.

Decisions (11)

Between two words
choose the quieter one.

Between word and silence
choose listening.

Between two books
choose the dustier one.

Between the earth and the sky
choose a bird.

Between two animals
choose the one who needs you more.

Between two children
choose both.

Between the lesser and the bigger evil
choose neither.

Between hope and despair
choose hope:
it will be harder to bear.

Boris A Novak
Translated from the Slovenian by Mia Dintinjana

Boris A Novak (born 1953) is a Slovene poet, playwright and translator and
has published 15 books. Novak also writes for children and edits a literary
magazine for children, *Kurirèek* (*The Little Messenger*).

Being an Artist

I perform with broken ribs
caught up in a sugar stampede
bruised by batons
stomped by booted feet
A running nose
remnants of teargas
in my nasal passages
I stand on shaky feet
having walked into town
A crowded bus for the return journey
buttocks of someone's wife against my groin
I stand dizzy
A packet of *maputi* for lunch
The water is dirty
I have diarrhoea
I stink
have learnt to bathe with a litre of water
The smell of smoke
cooking on a thorny bush fire
I stand here and talk about it
I will be accused of being an imperialist stooge
I need a bulletproof vest
They will graduate from batons to guns
After I am gone I won't rest
They will set up roadblocks
harass the mourners
and ask 'Where is your police clearance?'

Mgcini Nyoni

Mgcini Nyoni (born 1979) is a Zimbabwean poet, playwright and screenwriter
who recently changed his name from Shepherd Mandhlazi.
Maputi is popped maize.

The History of Morality

You've mounted me and there you sit,
you rotten shit!
You've mounted me and there you sit,
but even that won't really make
me think like you.

For the horse thinks one way as he strides;
thoughts quite different from the one who rides.

Alexandre O'Neill
Translated from the Portuguese by Alexis Levitin

Alexandre O'Neill (1924-86) was a leading figure in Portuguese Surrealism with several volumes of verse to his credit. His playful and satirical poetry reflected a conflicted relationship with his country, particularly under the dictatorial regime of António de Oliveira Salazar (1932-68).

Municipal Gum

Gumtree in the city street,
Hard bitumen around your feet,
Rather you should be
In the cool world of leafy forest halls
And wild bird calls.
Here you seems to me
Like that poor cart-horse
Castrated, broken, a thing wronged,
Strapped and buckled, its hell prolonged,
Whose hung head and listless mien express
Its hopelessness.
Municipal gum, it is dolorous
To see you thus
Set in your black grass of bitumen –
O fellow citizen,
What have they done to us?

Oodgeroo of the tribe Noonuccal

Oodgeroo of the tribe Noonuccal (1920-93) was a writer, painter and political activist who was born Kath Walker. She resumed her traditional name and returned an MBE (Member of the British Empire medal) in protest at the condition of her people during Australia's Bicentenary. 'My name is Oodgeroo from the tribe of the Noonuccal, custodian of the land that the white man calls Stradbroke Island and that the Aboriginal people call Minjerriba.'

Oodgeroo worked as a domestic servant after leaving school aged 13. Her debut collection *We Are Going* (1964) made her the first published Aboriginal woman and sold out in three days.

Oodgeroo was involved in many Aboriginal rights organizations and her poetry gave voice to a spectrum of human and environmental rights concerns. She spent her last days on Stradbroke Island, where she established a cultural and environmental education centre known as Moongalba (Resting-place).

Draft of a Reparations Agreement

All right, gentlemen who cry blue murder as always,
nagging miracle-makers,
quiet!
Everything will be returned to its place,
paragraph after paragraph.
The scream back into the throat.
The gold teeth back to the gums.
The terror.
The smoke back to the tin chimney and further on and inside
back to the hollow of the bones,
and already you will be covered with skin and sinews and you
will live,
look, you will have your lives back,
sit in the living room, read the evening paper.
Here you are. Nothing is too late.
As to the yellow star:
it will be torn from your chest
immediately
and will emigrate
to the sky.

Dan Pagis
Translated from the Hebrew by Stephen Mitchell

Dan Pagis (1930-86) was an Israeli poet and critic whose work has been widely
translated. Born in Romania, he had as a child been interned in a concentration
camp in the Ukraine for several years.
    The 'yellow star' is an age-old symbol of the hatred and persecution of
Jewish people. In the Middle Ages Jews were made to wear cloth patches of
the yellow star on their clothing to identify them, a practice that was revived
by the Nazis.

The Road Back

Starting on the frosty path at dawn,
mother now soaked from the heavy night's dew;
mother has come back after a day of selling
to the place where we lie asleep.

There is no jar of honey on the shelf,
only the gray dust piling,
while the children, too small to work
off the debts, lie stretching here, there.

No one to see, no one
to comprehend when she unties
the starlight she carries back on her forehead,
and shakes loose the moonlight
that clings to her sleeves.

Pak Chaesam

Translated from the Korean by David R McCann and Jiwon Shin

Pak Chaesam (1933-97) came from an impoverished family and lived most of his life in the same seaside town in South Korea. He remains something of a literary outsider in Korean literature and struggled financially throughout his life.

Practice for Hangmen

When the world is filled with evil,
Transform all mishaps into the path of bodhi.
– The Mind-Training Slogans of Atisha

The Egyptian forensic doctor Fakhri Ohamed Saleh told the Arab
television network Al-Jazeera that on rare occasions, a hanging
can accidentally cause decapitation, due to bad quality rope or
executioners who lack experience.
-Reuters, 15 January 2007

1. Get as much experience as you can.

2. Black goes with everything.

3. Learn the ropes.

4. Hang out with famous people.

5. The bigger they come, the harder they fall.

6. Never speak ill of the dead.

7. Always meditate on whatever provokes resentment.

8. You have the last word.

9. Don't tell the children.

10. The lighter the body, the longer the drop.

11. Blood is thicker than water.

12. Boil noose for one (1) hour.

13. Practice makes perfect.

14. Place knot directly behind left ear.

15. Maintain a joyful mind.

16. Lubricant may prevent tissue damage at neck.

17. Don't expect applause.

18. This is a thankless job.

19. Dead men have no friends.

20. Never say die.

21. Somebody has to do the dirty work.

22. No special training required.

23. Turn off all cell phones.

24. The fear of death is worse than death itself.
25. Enjoy the gallows' humor.
28. Your only function is to release a trap door.
29. Out of sight, out of mind.
30. When you go home, wipe yr feet.
31. Avoid talking shop.
32. Never lose yr head.

Ambar Past
Translated from the Spanish by Munda Tostón

Ambar Past (born 1949) became fascinated by books at an early age, composing her first book of poems by the age of 7 and working in print shops from the age of 11. At 23, Past emigrated to Mexico from the US and became a Mexican citizen. She has lived for 30-odd years in rural communities in the highlands of Chiapas, where she learnt Tzotzil Mayan and has translated ritual poetry from that language. She has published several chapbooks of her own verse in Spanish and founded *La Jicara*, a journal for art and literature. She has done a variety of jobs and travelled widely.

Aída Cartagena Portalatín (1918-94) was one of the Dominican Republic's best-loved poets, whose work took on big themes such as colonialism and imperialism, in a voice that was philosophical yet grounded in historical reality. She was a university professor and also published fiction and essays. In 1981 she published a book-length poem, *Yania Tierra*, which encapsulated the history of the Dominican Republic through the voice of its eponymous female protagonist.

Second Elegy
(Fragment)

My mother was one of the great mothers
of the world.
From her womb were born seven children who would be
in Dallas, Memphis, or Birmingham
a racial question.
(Neither black nor white.)
Lala, who kept her house for thirty years,
does not forget her and each time
the cold wind comes down our valley
those who were given her light, warm blankets
remember her too.
Mama knew nothing of political theory
(papal encyclicals or Karl Marx).
She only understood that the poor suffered hunger,
begged bread, needed shelter.
One lady journalist called her
a one woman programme for social assistance.
And now women of virtuous lives and those
who missed the straight path
miss her sorely.
Her acts were the duties of love.
Mama. Olimpia. Mama.
The public should not raise monuments
to sacks of groceries, blankets, roofs.
Such things are the duties of love.

Aída Cartagena Portalatín
Translated from the Spanish by Emma Jane Robinett

We Will Return One Day

One day we will return to our homeland
snug and warm in our hopes.
We will return no matter how much time goes by,
no matter how great the distance,
so please, heart, do not cave in along the way.
How it hurts to see the flocks of birds returning
without us.
Behind the hills are hills that sleep and wake to our promise
and people for whom waiting is love and a sad song,
lands whose willows fill the whole horizon
bending to any water.
In their shade tiny flowers gulp
serene perfume, immaculate joy.
We will return: the nightingale told me
the bulbuls still feed
on our poetry
and there is still a place for us
between the yearning hills
and the yearning people.
Oh, heart, no matter how far the winds scatter us
we will return to our homeland.

Harun Hashim Rasheed

Translated from the Arabic by Saadi Simawe and Ellen Doré Watson

Harun Hashim Rasheed (born 1927) is a Palestinian poet who, as a child
in Gaza, witnessed British soldiers demolishing his home in reprisal against
Palestinian rebels. His Palestinian identity is a key theme in his poetry:
'Palestinian is my name./ In a clear script,/ On all battlefields,/ I have inscribed
my name,/ Eclipsing all other titles.'

Vicki Raymond (born 1949) lived in Tasmania until coming to London in
1981. Her poetry's essential quality is its wit.
   The title of this poem is an inversion of Carl Sandburg's famous
'The People, Yes' which is a paean to the heroism of working people.

The People, No

You never hear 'the People' now:
that thundering, slightly frightening sea
has been oiled flat.
But 'people' you hear everywhere,
a baby chirrup sensuously drawn out.

The People used to be a little
too fond of crowds for their own good.
Like movie extras, they
were sent from place to place, kept standing
long hours in the sun and, finally,
given their fortnight's pay.

People, on the other hand,
were sensitive, and cared;
and they agreed they needed
to keep their weight down, running
around the park each morning.
No wonder that they superseded

that poor old dinosaur, the People,
who smoked, and never understood
that to survive you have to be quite small,
and sometimes seem not to be there at all.

Let's hear it, then, for people,
their sensitivity and taste,
their sets of values
like sets of willow pattern,
so delicate, so easily replaced.

Vicki Raymond

Filipenza

In the modern Greek dictionary, the word 'Filipenza' means 'maid'.

If I became the brown woman mistaken
for a shadow, please tell your people I'm a tree.
Or its curling root above the ground, like fingers without a rag,

without the buckets of thirst to wipe clean your mirrorlike floors.
My mother warned me about the disappearance of Elena.
But I left her and told her it won't happen to me.

The better to work here in a house full of faces I don't recognize.
Shame is less a burden if spoken in the language of soap and stain.
My whole country cleans houses for food, so that

the cleaning ends with the mothers, and the daughters
will have someone clean for them, and never leave
my country to spend years of conversations with dirt.

When I get up, I stand like a tree, feet steady, back firm.
From here, I can see Elena's island, where she bore a child
by a married man whose floors she washed for years,

whose body stained her memory until she left in the thick
of rain, unseen yet now surviving in the uncertain tongues
of the newly arrived. Like the silence in the circling motions

of our hands, she becomes part myth, part mortal, part soap.

Bino A Realuyo

Bino A Realuyo was born and raised in Manila in the Philippines and came to the US as a teenager when his family moved. He is a novelist, poet, community organizer and adult educator. He has worked with labour unions in New York City.

The Philippines is a prime supplier of migrant labour to other parts of the world. Many young Filipinas go overseas to work in often hellish conditions as domestic workers. Apart from economic pressures, the traditional low status of women in many parts of Filipino society is a prominent push factor.

Wanderer

I graze all over these arching slopes.
Up your breast I climb,
Plant my lips on the pinnacle.
The pink trail of teeth proves I am the first
To come this way.

I skate from hipbone to hipbone.
Descend past your navel
To the whirlpool's rim.
My tongue, slow, cunning,
Writhes to the crevice,
Falls stunned in the wet valley,
Turning there like a child in its bed.
You devour my fist
Up to the knuckle.
The earth heaves
Again. And again.

Rekha

This poem, with its exultant eroticism, first appeared in a groundbreaking book *Facing the Mirror: Lesbian Writing from India* published in 1999 by the Indian imprint of Penguin. It was the first such collection of lesbian voices from the country and most of the contributors (including **Rekha** above) chose the anonymity of a single name. No biographical details were included.

This is all of a piece with the taboo around minority sexualities in the country, which is bolstered by a colonial law, Section 377, that criminalizes 'carnal intercourse against the order of nature'. Although rarely enforced, the law lays LGBT people open to blackmail, often by corrupt police officials, and bolsters prejudice. Section 377 is being challenged in the Delhi High Courts.

In recent years, particularly with growing internet activism, the Indian queer community is becoming more visible. There have been numerous media articles condemning the archaic law and in 2008 the first Queer Pride marches happened in some of the major cities, many of the participants wearing rainbow-coloured masks.

Akleema

Akleema,
the sister of Cain and Abel,
is born of the same mother
but she is different.
Different between her thighs
and in the bulge of her breasts
Different in her gut
and inside her womb
Why is the fate of all of these
the sacrifice of a fatted lamb?

Imprisoned by her own body
burning in the scalding sun
She stands on a hilltop
like a mark etched on stone
Look at this mark carefully
above the long thighs
above the high breasts
above the tangled womb
Akleema has a head too
Let God speak to Akleema sometime
And ask her something.

Fahmida Riaz

Translated from the Urdu by Rukhsana Ahmad

Fahmida Riaz (born 1946) is a Pakistani poet and feminist. During her editorship of *Awaaz* (Voice), 14 court cases for sedition were filed against the magazine, one of the charges carrying the death penalty. She escaped to India while on bail and spent much of the 1980s there. She returned to Pakistan upon the restoration of democracy under Benazir Bhutto's Pakistan People's Party.

She has published several volumes of her poetry and caused a furore with her frank explorations of women's sexuality in *Badan Dareeda* (*The Lacerated Body*).

A version of the Cain and Abel story has it that the brothers fought over their sister Akleema's hand.

The Eye

A balcony, violet shade on stucco   fruit in a plastic bowl on the iron
    raggedy legged table, grapes and sliced melon, saucers, a knife, wine
in a couple of thick short tumblers cream cheese once came in: our snack
    in the eye of the war   There are places where fruit is implausible, even
rest is implausible, places where wine if any should be poured into
                      wounds
    but we're not yet there or it's not here yet   it's the war
not us, that moves, pauses and hurtles forward into the neck
    and groin of the city, the soft indefensible places but not here yet

Behind the balcony an apartment, papers, pillows, green vines
                    still watered
    there are waterless places but not here yet, there's a bureau
                topped with marble
and combs and brushes on it, little tubes for lips and eyebrows,
                a dish of coins and keys
    there's a bed a desk a stove a cane rocker a bookcase civilization
cage with a skittery bird, there are birdless places but not
    here yet, this bird must creak and flutter in the name of all
uprooted orchards, limbless groves
    this bird standing for wings and song that here can't fly

Our bed quilted   wine poured   future uncertain   you'd think
    people like us would have it scanned and planned tickets to somewhere
would be in the drawer with all our education you'd think we'd have
                taken measures
    soon as ash started turning up on the edges of everything ash
in the leaves of books ash on the leaves of trees and in the veins
                of the passive
    innocent life we were leading calling it hope

you'd think that and we thought this   it's the war not us that's moving
  like shade on a balcony

Adrienne Rich

Adrienne Rich (born 1929) is among the most influential American poets
of her generation. Her championing of feminist and lesbian issues has been
inspirational. Her anti-war activism goes back to the 1960s. She has written
several books of verse for which she has received numerous major awards.
    Refusing the National Medal of Arts in 1997 from the Clinton
Administration she declared that art 'means nothing if it simply decorates the
dinner table of the power which holds it hostage'.

The Fairies Are Dancing
All Over the World

The fairies are dancing all over the world
    In the dreams of the President
        they are dancing
  although he dares not mention this at cabinet meetings
In the baby blood of the brandnew
    they are dancing O most rapturously
and over the graves of the fathers and mothers
      who are dead
and around the heads of the mothers and fathers who are not dead
    in celebration of the sons and daughters
      they've given the earth
The fairies are dancing in the paws and muzzles
    of dogs larking in the broad field next to the church
The fairies have always danced in the blood of the untamed
      in the muscular horned goat
    and the shining snake
  in the blood of Henry Thoreau
    and most certainly Emily Dickinson
And they skip in the blood of the marine recruit
    in his barracks at night
        his bones aching with fatigue and loneliness
    and pure dreams of women
          and his goodbuddy in the next bunk
They are most lovely in the eyes of the black kid
    trucking in front of the jukebox
    at the local pizzeria,
more timorous in the eyes of his white friend
    whose hips are a bit more calcified
with hereditary denunciation of the fairies
    May the fairies swivel his hips
On sap green evenings in early summer

the fairies danced under the moon in country places
danced among native american teepees
and hung in the rough hair of buffalos racing across the prairies
and are dancing still
most hidden
and everywhere
In some, only in the eyes
in others a reach of the arm
a sudden yelp of joy
reveals their presence
The fairies are dancing from coast to coast
all over deadmiddle America
they're bumping and grinding on the Kremlin walls
the tap of their feet is eroding all the walls
all over the world as they dance
In the way of the western world
the fairies' dance has become small
a bleating, crabbed jerkiness
but there for all that,
a bit of healthy green in the dead wood
that spreads an invisible green fire
around and around the globe
encircling it in its dance
of intimacy with the secret of all living things
The fairies are dancing even in the Pope's nose
and in the heart of the most stubborn macho
who will not and will not
and the fairies will
most insistently
because he will not
In the Pentagon the fairies are dancing
under the scrambled egg hats
of those who see no reason why youths should live to old age
The fairies bide their time and wait
They dance in invisible circlets of joy

around and around and over the planet
they are the green rings unseen by spaceships
their breath is the earth of the first spring evening
They explode in the black buds of deadwood winter
Welcome them with open arms
They are allies courting in the bloodstream
welcome them and dance with them

Michael Rumaker

Michael Rumaker (born 1932) is principally known as a short story writer,
a novelist whose work has often dealt with themes of gay male identity and a
memoirist. The poem printed here first appeared in *Gay Sunshine* in 1975 and
hasn't stopped dancing since, with inclusion in numerous anthologies.

In a recent interview he talked about his view of the political themes of his
work: 'Preachy and teachy harangues quickly grow old, but the political – by
which I mean real human lives not abstractions as so much politics is today –
has always been a vital aspect of our daily lives. Is it possible to get the political
into our words, that long and lively tongue of language through the ages, the
tongue that knows that words are tasty in the mouth?'

He has taught at City College, New York, and Rockland Community
College, also in New York.

The True Prison

It is not the leaking roof
Nor the singing mosquitoes
In the damp, wretched cell.
It is not the clank of the key
As the warder locks you in.
It is not the measly rations
Unfit for man or beast
Nor yet the emptiness of day
Dipping into the blankness of night
It is not
It is not
It is not
It is the lies that have been drummed
Into your ears for one generation
It is the security agent running amok
Executing callous calamitous orders
In exchange for a wretched meal a day
The magistrate writing in her book
Punishment she knows is undeserved
The moral ineptitude
Mental decrepitude
Lending dictatorship spurious legitimacy
Cowardice asked as obedience.
Lurking in our denigrated souls
It is fear damping trousers
We dare not wash off our urine
It is this
It is this

It is this

Dear friend, turns our free world

Into a dreary prison.

Ken Saro-Wiwa

Kenule 'Ken' Beeson Saro-Wiwa (1941-95) was a Nigerian author, television producer, and environmentalist. He was also a spokesperson for the Movement of the Survival of the Ogoni People based in the Niger Delta, an area facing environmental devastation and human rights abuses related to oil exploration and extraction by transnational companies, especially Shell. Saro-Wiwa was first imprisoned by the Nigerian authorities for his activism and then executed, his death bringing increased international attention to the struggle of the Ogoni people.

In June 2009, Shell settled a lawsuit by agreeing to pay $15.5 million to the families of Saro-Wiwa and others who had charged the oil giant with collusion with the Nigerian authorities, including the supplying of weapons. Shell made the payment without admitting to any wrongdoing.

Burmese poet **Saw Wai** was arrested on 22 January 2008 and subsequently sentenced to two years for this seemingly innocuous love poem that tells of the heartbreak of a suitor rejected by a 'photomodel'. However, in Burmese, the first words of each line when read from top to bottom spell out the message 'Power Crazy Madman Senior General Than Shwe'. Than Shwe leads the military junta that runs Burma with an iron hand, cracking down on all dissent and keeping political opponents incarcerated. The most famous of these is the Nobel Peace Prize winner Aung San Suu Kyi, who has spent 13 years under house arrest and is imprisoned and on trial at the time of writing because a US tourist swam across a lake to her house to visit her. Former political prisoners speak of appalling conditions and torture. The regime also has a habit of summarily extending sentences on the anticipated day of release.

Burmese censorship is strict and it was the ingenious device used in this poem by Saw Wai that got it past the censors. Knowledge of the secret message makes it open to interpretation beyond the soppy love scenario it outlines. What, for example, are we to make of the laughing and clapping millions 'who know how to love' evoked in the closing lines? An image of optimism and defiance?

Saw Wai is primarily known for his romantic poetry and is also a performance artist. Before his arrest he headed the White Rainbow group of artists and writers in Burma who raised money for children orphaned by the AIDS crisis in the country.

Aaron Beck is the creator of cognitive therapy and has done extensive work on depression and anxiety. The Beck Depression Inventory is one of the most widely used measures of depression severity.

'a broken liver': the Burmese way of saying 'a broken heart'.

February 14

Ar rin bek ka pyaw dair
  Aaron Beck, the psychiatrist, said
Nar nar khan sah dat hma khan sah hma
  Only if you know how to suffer painfully
Yoo yoo moo moo go phyit nay hma
  Only if you are crazy – crazy
Kyi myat tet a noot pyinnya lo
  Can you appreciate a great work of Art
Hmoo hmoan hmaing way zay det dat poan model ma lay yay
  Dear little photomodel who makes me dizzy
Kyi daunk kyi mah kya hma a thair kwair det yawgah det
  They say it is a broken liver disease, a great and terrible one
Than baung myah zwa thaw chit tat thu myah
  Millions of those who know how to love
Shwe a teet cha hta thaw let myah phyint let khoak tee yway
                                                    yair bar
  Laugh and clap those gold-gilded hands

Saw Wai
Translated from the Burmese by David Law

Passover 2002

Instead of scalding
your pots and plates,
take steel wool
to your hearts:
You read the Haggadah
like swine, which
if put before a table
would forage about in the bowl
for parsley and dumplings.
Passover, however,
is stronger than you are.
Go outside and see:
the slaves are rising up,
a brave soul
is burying its oppressor
beneath the sand.
Here is your cruel,
stupid Pharaoh,
dispatching his troops
with their chariots of war,
and here is the Sea of Freedom,
which swallows them.

Aharon Shabtai
Translated from the Hebrew by Peter Cole

Aharon Shabtai (born 1939) is among Israel's foremost poets, with 16 published poetry collections and a distinguished career as Hebrew's leading translator of classical Greek drama. The boldness of his themes (from unabashed eroticism to excoriating political engagement), expressed in uncompromising, muscular verse, has given rise to considerable controversy.

Many of Shabtai's poems were first published in the literary pages of the weekend edition of Israel's most credible newspaper, *Ha'aretz*, where they have often provoked angry correspondence and cancelled subscriptions. 'Passover 2002' appeared in *Ha'aretz* days before the festival, which is one of the most joyous celebrations of the Jewish calendar. Traditional Jewish families either use separate kitchen utensils for the holiday or make their ordinary utensils kosher, usually by immersing them in boiling water.

The poem's date places it within the context of the escalating violence and insecurity of the region at a time when hardliner Ariel Sharon was at the helm and the second Palestinian intifada (uprising) was intense. Translator Peter Cole in his introduction to *J'Accuse*, an English language collection of Shabtai's poetry, has noted: 'What drives [Shabtai] to his desk … is the understanding that the fate of the ethical Hebrew culture in which he was raised is inextricably linked to the fate of Palestinian society and the Palestinian people, which his own government is doing its best to crush.'

The Haggadah is a Jewish religious text that sets out the order of the Passover ritual and involves the 'telling' (the literal meaning of Haggadah) of the Jewish liberation from slavery in Egypt, as described in the book of Exodus. The Sea of Freedom is where injustice drowns; it swallowed up Pharoah's pursuing army in the Exodus story.

In This Dead-End

They smell your mouth
lest you should have said: 'I love you.'
They smell your heart.
What a strange world, my dear!

And they whip love
near the lampposts.
We must hide love in the closet.

In this zig-zag dead-end of coldness
they keep the fire alive
with song and poetry.
Do not be afraid of thinking.
Whoever knocks at the door at night
has come to kill the light.
We must hide light in the closet.

Now the butchers are
on each cross-road
with a tree trunk and a bloody cleaver.
What a strange world, my dear!
And they operate to put a smile on our lips
and a song in our mouths.
We must hide our pleasures in the closet.

They barbecue canaries on fire
made of lilies and lilacs.
What a strange world, my dear!

It is the triumphant drunkard Devil

who is celebrating our sorrow.
We must hide God in the closet.

Ahmad Shamlu
Translated from the Persian by Gholam Reza Sami Gorgan Roodi

Ahmad Shamlu (1925-2000) was Iran's most celebrated 20th-century poet and for many Iranians a symbol of secular nationalism. Shamlu faced suppression of his work, which was always politically engaged, throughout his career. Nevertheless he produced over 70 books during his lifetime: poetry, children's literature, novels, short stories, screenplays and translations.

In 1970 he was exiled by the Shah. He led a secular intellectual movement against the Shah's dictatorship with other prominent Iranians. But with the overthrow of the Shah and the institution of the religious regime, Shamlu's hopes of freedom were not realized. This poem was written shortly after the institution of the theocratic regime and its many restrictions.

The Dance

In a field of cinders where Armenian life
was still dying,
a German woman, trying not to cry
told me of the horror she witnessed:

'This thing I'm telling you about,
I saw with my own eyes.
Behind my window of hell
I clenched my teeth
and watched the town of Bardez turn
into a heap of ashes.
The corpses were piled high as trees,
and from the springs, from the streams and the road,
the blood was a stubborn murmur,
and still calls revenge in my ear.

Don't be afraid; I must tell you what I saw,
so people will understand
the crimes men do to men.
For two days, by the road to the graveyard...

Let the hearts of the world understand,
it was Sunday morning,
the first useless Sunday dawning on the corpses.
From dawn to dusk I had been in my room
with a stabbed woman –
my tears wetting her death –
when I heard from afar
a dark crowd standing in a vineyard
lashing twenty brides
and singing filthy songs.

Leaving the half-dead girl on the straw mattress,
I went to the balcony of my window
and the crowd seemed to thicken like a clump of trees.
An animal of a man shouted, "You must dance,
dance when our drum beats".
With fury whips cracked
on the flesh of the women.
Hand in hand the brides began their circle dance.
Now, I envied my wounded neighbour
because with a calm snore she cursed
the universe and gave up her soul to the stars...

"Dance," they raved,
"dance till you die, infidel beauties
with your flapping tits, dance!
Smile for us. You're abandoned now,
you're naked slaves,
so dance like a bunch of fuckin' sluts.
We're hot for your dead bodies."
Twenty graceful brides collapsed.
"Get up," the crowd screamed,
brandishing their swords.

Then someone brought a jug of kerosene.
Human justice, I spit in your face.
The brides were anointed.
"Dance," they thundered –
"here's a fragrance you can't get in Arabia."

With a torch, they set
the naked brides on fire.
And the charred bodies rolled

and tumbled to their deaths...

I slammed my shutters,
sat down next to my dead girl
and asked: "How can I dig out my eyes?"'

Siamanto
Translated from the Armenian by Peter Balakian and Nevart Yaghlian

Siamanto (Atom Yarjanian, 1878-1915) was born in the town of Akn (formerly
within the Ottoman Empire, now Kemaliye, Turkey). Primarily a writer of
epic poems, he also brought the difficult subject of genocide into verse. He
used blunt language to express the suffering of the Armenian people during
massacres perpetrated by the Ottoman army in 1895-96 and 1909. In 1915,
Siamanto was one of a group of Armenian intellectuals rounded up for
deportation to Anatolia and slaughtered on the way.

That year marks the beginning of the genocidal killings of Armenian (and
Anatolian and Greek) people by the Ottoman Empire, which were carried
out under the wings of the First World War. It is estimated that one and a half
million Armenians were murdered as a result.

It is claimed that when Hitler embarked on his plans to eliminate Jewish
people in Nazi Germany he referred to how the world had forgotten the
Armenian holocaust. Turkey insists no genocide took place. When the US
Congress was considering officially recognizing the Armenian genocide,
Turkey threatened the closure of US bases in the country. Turkish intellectuals
who have raised the issue have faced persecution and prosecution.

A Scene, After the War

I'd never been aware how beautiful my house is
until I saw it burning,
my schoolmate told me, who had twenty pieces of shrapnel
that remained deep under his skin after the war.
He wrote me how at the airport he enjoyed
having upset the customs officials who couldn't understand
why the checkpoint metal detector howled for no reason.

I had never been aware I was a nation
until they said they'd kill me,
my friend told me,
who'd escaped from a prison camp
only to be caught and raped by Gypsies
while she was roaming in the woods.
Then they sold her to some Italian pimps
who tattooed the owner's brand and number on her fist.
She says you cannot see it when she wears gloves.

I recognized them in a small town in Belgium.
They were sitting and watching the river
carry plastic bags, cans,
and garbage from the big city.
She was caressing the hard shrapnel lumps
through his shirt
and he was caressing her glove.

I wanted to say hello
and give them a jolly photograph from the times
when none of us knew the meaning
of House and Nation.

Then I realized that there was more meaning
in the language of silence
in which they were seeing off
the plastic bags down the river
than in the language
in which I would have tried to feign those faces
from the old photograph
that shows us all smiling long ago.

Goran Simić

Translated from the Serbian by Amela Simić

Goran Simić (born 1952) is one of the pre-eminent literary figures of the
former Yugoslavia, and has published several volumes of poetry, short-stories,
plays and literary criticism. He was caught in the siege of Sarajevo (1992-
96) during the Bosnian War when the inhabitants of the city became targets.
Around 10,000 people died or were missing by the end of the siege. Simić lost
his mother and brother.

He has spoken of being named an 'ideological traitor' because his writings
strove to keep the 'idea of a multi-religious and multinational Bosnia alive',
and of Sarajevo, once the proud host of the Winter Olympics, reduced to an
'ashtray' after the siege. In 1996 he was able to emigrate to Canada under the
auspices of Canadian PEN and remains an active PEN member.

Portuguese Mistake

When the Portuguese came
In a heavy rain
He dressed the Indian.
Pity!
If it had been a sunny morning
The Indian would have stripped
The Portuguese.

José Oswald de Andrade Souza
Translated from the Portuguese by Régis Bonvicino and Douglas Messerli

José Oswald de Andrade Souza (1890-1954) was a poet, polemicist and social agitator. One of the Founders of Brazilian modernism, he argued that Brazil's history of 'cannibalizing' other cultures was its greatest strength and a bulwark against European cultural domination.

The Snapshot Album
of the Innocent Tourist

This is a space for the President's
Rather splendid Palace,
Standing above
The not-so-picturesque
Riverflat shanties.
'Prohibido!' said the baby-faced boy
Whose gun was real,
'Prohibido!': I got the message
If not the shot.

This is a space for the corner
Where the student was beaten to death
And for the feet of workers
Stepping, they said, at morning
Round a pool of blood.
I couldn't focus it
For Christmas traffic
And besides it looked
Like any intersection, anywhere.

This space is for twenty working years
Erased from the centre
Of a teacher's life.
'It's good to be back,' he says
And smiles as if believing
The text can be restored:
All its pages,
The ungiven lectures, the burnt books,
The silenced words.

This is the space for the disbelief

Of the elegant woman
Whose perfume is charming
Like her apartment.
Only the tiniest hairline scar
Betrays the facial tuck, the will to deny:
'It was terrible,' she cries
'But nobody knew. Nobody spoke.
How could we know?'

This space is for the grandparents
Who hid a dangerous child,
Unregistered,
Infected by his father,
Who died 'resisting arrest,' his mother
Who left for a meeting
And never came back,
Except in the set of his mouth
When the boy is angry, or laughs.

This is a space for all the disappeared
Who fade in other people's albums:
This is a space for courage
And for love,
For things that don't show up
In negatives.

Jennifer Strauss

Australian poet **Jennifer Strauss** (born 1933) has had a long academic career
and has edited anthologies of verse and published four volumes of her own
poetry. She is Honorary Senior Research Fellow at Monash University. In 2007
Strauss was awarded the Medal of the Order of Australia for her work in the
fields of education, literature and poetry and for her work in women's issues
and industrial relations.

Letters from Exile

These are the letters I leave behind me,
dull lines written for the censor's eye.
There are no stories here, only headlines,
statements of fact, shielding the truth.

But how can I write my life without politics
when each word placed is part of an equation?
Talk of my income will be translated
into an exact amount for blackmail or ransom;
Talk of our culture will be interpreted
as a covert call to arms.

I cannot tell you
that I am learning our language,
that I stand as a poet on a Western stage
crying out the loss of our country.

I cannot send you
photographs or cassette tapes.
You will not see my hair turn gray
or my voice change accent
as I become American.

I cannot even send you postcards
because such pictures
are considered currency in our country
and will go home with the postman
to be traded for food.

I write these words for you
knowing the line of people that stand between us:
my cousin, who will sit beside you, translating,

the villagers, hoping for news of their families,
and the government clerk, who will slit open
this letter, like all the others,
checking each word, over and over,
the most sensitive audience I could ask for.

Pireeni Sundaralingam

Pireeni Sundaralingam was born and raised in Sri Lanka, educated at Oxford, and now lives in San Francisco. Her poetry concentrates on the many facets of the exile experience. She has edited the first anthology of South Asian American poetry, *Writing the Lines of Our Hands*. Her own first poetry collection, *Flotsam and Jetsam*, is forthcoming.

Psalm

How leaky are all the borders
we draw around our separate nations!
How many clouds cross those boundaries
daily without even paying the toll!
How much desert sand
simply sifts from country to country,
or how many mountain pebbles
hop down slopes onto foreign turf just like that!

Need I remind you of each and every bird
as it flies over, and now sits,
on a closed border-gate?
Even if it's small as a sparrow, its tail is abroad
while its beak is still at home.
And if that weren't enough, it keeps fidgeting!

Out of countless insects, I will single out the ant,
who, right between the guard's left boot
and his right, pays no attention to any questions of origin or
destination.

If only this whole messy affair
could be studied more, in detail,
all around the world!
Look! Isn't that familiar hedge on the far bank even now
smuggling its hundred-thousandth leaf
over the river?

And who else but the squid, unashamed
of the length of its arms, would violate
the precious boundary of our territorial waters?

How can we speak
of any semblance of order around here
when we can't even rearrange the stars
to show which one shines for whom?

Not to mention the fog,
which reprehensively goes wherever it pleases. Or that dust
　　　　　　　　　　　　　blowing blithely all over the prairie
as if the land had never been partitioned.
And the voices gliding on the obliging airwaves! All these
　　　　　　　　　　　　　conspiratorial gurglings
and suggestive sounds.

Funny, isn't it, how only what's human is truly alien? Everything
　　　　　　　　　　　　　else is just mixed vegetation,
a few subversive moles, and the wind.

Wisława Szymborska
Translated by Mark Belletini

Wisława Szymborska (born 1923) is Poland's most celebrated poet and a 1996
winner of the Nobel Prize for Literature. Paradox and wit are the hallmarks of
her poetry, and those who know her personally remark on her modesty. In her
Nobel acceptance speech Szymborska reflected: 'Whatever inspiration is, it's
born from a continuous "I don't know".'

Thinking With the Body

At home inside your own skin,
As they say – while
Shielded by this paper cover
Lie the slow, tight coils of gut,
In sinuous unseen glitter
Of peristalsis, and the heart
Screaming outrage at the mile too swiftly
Run or the dismissive syllable.

Skin is the finishing touch, the sky-roof
Over this strangely autonomous
Realm and its sly imperfection
(Arrhythmia, or merely the stray
Kernel of corn tumbling toward
Some fæcal light, evading alimentation's
Unrelenting sweep, or the organized
Ugliness of ear and elbow); skin is all

We see: the creases in the open
Hand, that spell one's destiny:
Etched in a darkness that the eye's light
Cannot shape, the fœtal fist clutched
Tight round the last eternal shreds.

Does the soul live among the crackling
Sparkles, synapse to synapse,
Or in the coral memory,
Saline and submarine, like some
Sedentary beast, roiling gently
In the brain's convolutions –

Or in the cell's clever spirals,
Its geometries replicating the codes
Of immortality?

By your skins shall ye be known:
Life's sentence handed down
With shovel, brush, or in the straining rope's
Indelible characters, and the paper
Tautens, wrinkles, glows in the spray of salt
Wind and the cold of early winter; skin,
Skin is all

We can know of another's mind, heart.
Ache and rejoicing, how well we love
Ourselves: skin is where

Our names are written:
We write our own lines there.

Rowena Torrevillas

Rowena Torrevillas (born 1951) comes from a literary family and is twice winner of the Philippines' National Book Award. She teaches nonfiction writing and transnational literature at the University of Iowa.

The Tithe of War

I struggled in battle,
Won the war
And earned a rest.
My bones ploughed
The ground of peace.

It flowered and multiplied –
Watered with my sweat,
Fed with my flesh
And sweetened by my marrow.
The harvest was good.

Now I could sleep, content
With a blanket of earth,
Bushes for friends,
A mattress of dust
And a pillow of stones,

Except my spirit groans
When I hear you crying,
As you ululate and sing.
And when I see you crying
As you dance so proud.

I hear you, mother,
And I see your loved ones
Like a little wheat remaining
In the gleaned fields,
Or like a few raw seeds

When there's nothing left to eat.
Constantly hearing you cry
And seeing you in pain,
They think, *should we have survived?*
How will they go on?

Who gives a tithe
And asks for it back?
Mother, I paid it,
For you and all our freedom
Not to cry but live.

Solomon Tsehaye
Translated from the Tigrinya by Charles Cantalupo and Ghirmai Negash

Solomon Tsehaye (born 1956) is a poet, critic and the author of Eritrea's national anthem. The poem above appeared in its original Tigrinya language version in his 1994 collection *Sahel*. He has recently completed an authoritative book on traditional Eritrean oral poetry and poets.

The war that this poem refers to is Eritrea's 31-year war of independence and self-determination against neighbouring Ethiopia. Eritrea has suffered greatly from its colonial history, conquered first by Italy in 1890 and then subsequently taken over by the British in 1941. When the British left in 1951, Eritrea was federated with Ethiopia by a UN resolution. The Eritrean people, however, were not consulted, and resistance to the confederation was not long in coming. Ethiopia responded by annexing Eritrea as its 14th province in 1962. Eritrean culture was suppressed, and Amharic, the main Ethiopian language, was used in schools instead of languages such as Tigrinya (in which this poem was written) and Tigre which were the more widely spoken languages of the people.

After a long, armed struggle, Eritrean independence was won in 1993. Nonetheless, border issues with Ethiopia remain a source of tension. Many of the democratic principles contained in Eritrea's constitution have yet to be implemented, with political dissidents and religious minorities suffering repression.

Exile House

Our tiled roof dripped
and the four walls threatened to fall apart
but we were to go home soon.

We grew papayas
in front of our house
chillies in our garden
and changmas for our fences,
then pumpkins rolled down the cowshed thatch
calves trotted out of the manger.

Grass on the roof,
beans sprouted and
climbed the vines,
money plants crept in through the window,
our house seems to have grown roots.

The fences have grown into a jungle,
now how can I tell my children
where we came from?

Tenzin Tsundue

Tenzin Tsundue's parents fled Tibet in 1959 fearing persecution by the
Chinese authorities. He was born in a tent at a roadside while his parents
worked as road construction labourers in India, the exact date unknown. He is
a leading voice of the exile Tibetan community and his poetry has been widely
translated. He is also a daring campaigner for Tibetan independence, known for
his high-profile protests at the cost of great personal hardship. For the last eight
years he has worn a red bandana which he says he will remove only when Tibet
regains its freedom.
changma: a tree usually planted for fences: flexible and flourishing

Desert Years

Sobs
An intake of breath
A sliver of glass
Old decades of years
cannot consider
In these years the bees cannot
make honey the mushrooms
cannot sprout
All the fields are out of
crops. Dry.

The mist is damp
The storm is dim
Dust rising in clouds
Along the road where
the bullock cart
has traveled.

Encircled by thorns
the hta-naung tree its trunk
cat's-claw scratched is trying
to bloom.

It doesn't rain.

When it does – it's not enough
to soak the earth.

In the monastery at
the edge of the village
bells
are not heard. If they are

they do not enter the ears
blissfully.

There are no novices
orange-clad
zilch of sounds of young
voices
reciting the scriptures only the
kappiya attendant
with his
shaved head falls between the
pillars and columns of the
building.

The earth doesn't dare
to put forth fruit.
It abandons all
and looks at me
at once feeling embarrassed
and frightened as if she
cannot talk.

When will the sobs change
and the bells ring sweetly again?

U Tin Moe

Translated from the Burmese by Kyi May Kaung

(See page 162 for biographical note.)

Rafaela Padilla

I was going to the clandestine hospital
by the old Phoenix Cinema in Masaya
to give serum to a combatant
wounded in the Retreat.
There the guards
smashed me like a clay pot
with kicks and blows from their rifle butts.
Over the college steps that afternoon
spread a pool of my blood
and my sleek black hair.

I still resist blows, death,
I mind not minding the sick,
leaving my children motherless.
Hospital workers, Doctors, Nurses,
Comrades: our ancient human pain
is new, different and untransferable
in every patient. Remember that.
Don't ever forget.

Julio Valle-Castillo
Translated from the Spanish by Dinah Livingstone

Julio Valle-Castillo (born 1952) is a Nicaraguan poet, novelist, essayist, critic
and painter. This poem is infused with the spirit of the Sandinista struggle in
the country. The Sandinista National Liberation Front were a socialist political
grouping which first managed to overthrow the dictatorial Somoza dynasty in
1979 after a long insurrection and then had to face constant attack from the US-
sponsored Contras. However, during their 11 years in power, they succeeded
in broadening democratic participation in all matters of governance to an
unprecedented degree.

Hope (An Dochas)

Hope, dear heart, is nothing but
an impulse you do not control
and that you ought to unlearn.
You're like a child in front of the glittering
windows of a city store,
hungry, craving, and I'm your mother,
pulling you away, leading you back
to the dark, sad streets where our house is,
because I know we'll never be able
to buy those things, we have no chance
of ever owning or enjoying them.

Christopher Whyte
Translated from the Scottish Gaelic by the poet

Christopher Whyte (born 1952) is a Glaswegian poet (and champion of
Scottish poetry), translator and novelist who writes both in English and Scottish
Gaelic. He currently lives in Budapest, Hungary.

(See page 160) **U Tin Moe** (1933-2007), a poet laureate of Burma, fell from
grace with the military regime ruling the country during his involvement in
the pro-democracy movement in 1988. He was imprisoned for four years in the
notorious Insein jail and all his published works were banned in the country. He
left Burma in 1999 and died in California.

The poem uses metaphors of barrenness to illustrate the condition of the
country under the military dictatorship. The absence of novices in the scene
being described is significant: Buddhism is a mainstay of the people and
many young men spend at least part of their youth as novices in the numerous
monasteries. Poverty also forces many parents to pledge their young children to
the monasteries.

In recent years, joining a religious order has been a refuge for many young
people who need to go into hiding due to their political convictions. Monks
have a revered position in Burmese society and in September 2007 they led
a popular but short-lived uprising against the regime which has since been
dubbed the Saffron Revolution.

The Agreement

What shall we agree?
That we shall see each other again.
Where shall that be?
Where they let us.

What shall we do?
Whatever occurs to us.
What do we want?
What we have always wanted.

What we thought and weren't allowed to say.
What we saw but weren't allowed to see.
What we hoped for but didn't happen.
What we were and are no longer.

What shall we agree?
That we'll be there.

Wu Mei

Wu Mei is a Chinese poet who took part in the Tiananmen Square protests in China in 1989. Led mainly by students and intellectuals, the demonstrations occurred in a year that had seen the collapse of communist governments in other parts of the world. The protests were against the Government's authoritarianism, calling for market reform and democratic participation. There were also demonstrations in other parts of China.

After seven weeks, the authorities cleared the Square using tanks. The number of people killed was estimated at between 200 and 300 by the Chinese authorities, and between 2,000 and 3,000 by the Chinese Red Cross. There followed a crackdown on supporters of the demonstrators.

In Detention

He fell from the ninth floor
He hanged himself
He slipped on a piece of soap while washing
He hanged himself
He slipped on a piece of soap while washing
He fell from the ninth floor
He hanged himself while washing
He slipped from the ninth floor
He hung from the ninth floor
He slipped on the ninth floor while washing
He fell from a piece of soap while slipping
He hung from the ninth floor
He washed from the ninth floor while slipping
He hung from a piece of soap while washing.

Christopher van Wyk

Christopher van Wyk was born in Soweto, South Africa in 1957 and writes
children's books, novels and poetry. He has also written works especially aimed
at new readers.

Cradle rocking

Be little lambs, they tell us
So that when you grow up
We can lead you like sheep.

Can Yücel

Translated from the Turkish by Murat Nemet-Nejat

Can Yücel (1926-99) was one of Turkey's most distinguished 20th-century poets, who used language that was plain and often incorporated slang. He read Latin and Ancient Greek at Ankara and Cambridge universities and worked in the Turkish section of the BBC in the 1960s. He eventually returned to Turkey and translated Shakespeare, Lorca and Brecht into Turkish.

On the Desire for Precision

And then there was considerable exaggeration in the counting of

the corpses:

some counted a hundred, and others tallied four times that much;

one said he'd seen thirty burnt women

which his friend said was mistaken, there were only eleven,

and his error was intentional and political, not random,

and while I'm at it, he said, let me state for the record as well

that among the butchered there were only eight – two were shot,

and there's one instance in doubt, it's unclear

as to whether or not she was butchered, raped, or only slit open.

Also, with regard to the children, the last word hasn't been said:

everyone admits that six were crucified and one beaten

before his head was crushed, but who among us could maintain

that all who vanished without a trace,

or even some, were marched into the sea?

If so, how do we explain the bloodstains?

In matters like these, it's critical not to exaggerate;

one has to be sure to discriminate: at stake is the fate

of human beings who after all are liable to err in reports,

my learned friend, we've seen it before.

And so there was, that day, a monstrous debate,

though if not for the awful stench wafting up from the place

they'd have managed a perfectly accurate count, or come to blows,

who knows – the desire for precision is human no less

than the desire to slaughter, rape, crush, and obliterate

one's enemy or rival, a next-door neighbour or suspicious stranger,
or just each last ordinary man, woman, and child alive in the world.

Natan Zach

Translated from the Hebrew by Peter Cole

Natan Zach (born 1930) is among Israel's most prominent poets and has
been widely translated. His *Collected Poems* were recently published in three
volumes. He has, for many years now, worked for coexistence and protested
alongside Palestinian writers against the occupation of the territories.

Delighted With My Things

1

I am delighted because my hand is with me
delighted and joyous because my hand is still here
swinging at my side, so happy I raise it, wave to a young woman,
I let it drop, I say:
ahh! my freedom is here by my side
here, my heart
here, my shoulder shining like ebony with life's kisses

I'm delighted because the wind wet the evening and my shoulder
and shook my bed
Delighted and joyous am I because the hand that called to you
touched you
clasped you
is still with me

2

I am delighted by my voice, with its thick country accent
its giddiness
My voice is suitable for reciting, enticing, and singing –
                              especially when I'm drunk
Suitable for intimacy when I lose my bearings, and for Quranic
                              chanting and meditation
when meditation deserts its high tower
to gather daffodils for a woman

I'm thrilled when my voice decides to call to the friend
walking just for the heck of it on flowers
that wither to death.

I rejoice in my voice because it looks so much like me
It goes calm when I yearn or weep,
puts on old clothes when I embrace you,
and bursts out of me barefoot at night
to conform to the alphabet of your sleep.

3
Delighted with my things and my heart
Delighted with all my truths
and friends, though few and reluctant
Excited by the feel of your cheek, your voice
Thrilled by the magic of my sin and the ringing in my chest
Happy am I with what the world has done to me, and with what
my hands have done
to the world
I am delighted with my years

Ghassan Zaqtan
Translated from the Arabic by Saadi Simawe and Ellen Doré Watson

Ghassan Zaqtan (born 1954) spent his early years in the al-Karama refugee camp for Palestinians. In later life Zaqtan worked in Beirut until forced to leave in the Palestinian exodus that followed the Israeli invasion of Lebanon. He now lives in Ramallah and has ten books of poetry to his credit. He is regarded as an *avant garde* figure on the Arabic literary scene.

Love

How far my night is
                from your night!
Other nights rise between them like uncrossable mountains.

I sent the road out for you. But it didn't find you.
It grew weary and returned to me.
I sent out the roebuck of my song. But
The hunters shot it and, wounded,
                it returned to me.
I don't know which direction the wind took. It got lost
In the trees and in the caverns of pain, and returned to me, blinded.

Rain is falling, robbed of hope.

Tomorrow when day breaks, shall I send out a rainbow
To look for you? Though, as naïve as joy itself,
It can only cross one mountain.

I shall set out in the night myself.
I shall search, I shall search, I shall search
Like a hand groping in the darkness of a room,
            to find an extinguished candle.

Qafë-Bari prison camp, 1983

Visar Zhiti
Translated from the Albanian by Robert Elsie

Visar Zhiti (born 1952) had his early literary career blighted by the crackdown against intellectuals initiated by the Albanian Communist Party. In the mid-1970s he was singled out for blackening 'our socialist reality', probably because his father had come into conflict with the authorities. In 1979 he was finally arrested and sentenced the following year to ten years for 'agitation and propaganda', spending much of it in concentration camps – including the freezing mountain camp where this poem was composed.

He composed and memorized 97 poems during this period as pen and paper were forbidden. After the end of the communist dictatorship Zhiti's poetry gained recognition and today he is among Albania's most celebrated poets.

Thanks

Thanks are due to all the poets and translators who generously gave permission for the use of their work.
Thank you to Dexter Tiranti, who had the original idea for this book.
For the opening of doors, sincere thanks to:
David and Helen Constantine of *Modern Poetry in Translation*
Bas Kwakman and Marjolijn Abel of Poetry International
Charles Cantalupo
Peter Cole
Dinah Livingstone
and Adrienne Rich.
Thanks also to Bart Lienard for free secretarial assistance and constant support.

Dinyar Godrej
for New Internationalist and Amnesty International

Acknowledgements

The publishers would like to thank all copyright holders and rights managers listed below for their kind permission.

Chris Abani: 'Heavensgate'
from *Kalakuta Republic* © Chris Abani, 2000, first published by Saqi Books, London, 2000, by permission of Saqi Books

Kim Addonizio: 'Cranes in August'
from *The Philosopher's Club* (BOA editions, 1994), © Kim Addonizio. Used by permission of author.

Adonis: selections from 'The Desert'
Samih al-Qasim: 'The Story of a City'
Mahmud Darwish: 'The Earth is Closing on Us', all three translated by Abdullah al-Udhari
from *Victims of a Map*, © Abdullah al-Udhari, first published by Saqi Books, London, 1984, by permission of Saqi Books

Ama Ata Aidoo: 'Speaking of Hurricanes'
by permission of Ama Ata Aidoo

Anna Akhmatova: 'Epilogue', translated by Elaine Feinstein
published in *Modern Poetry in Translation*, Third Series Number 3, by permission of *Modern Poetry in Translation*

Elizabeth Alexander: 'Little Slave Narrative # 1: Master'
from *American Blue: Selected Poems* by Elizabeth Alexander (Bloodaxe Books, 2006), by permission of Bloodaxe Books and Abner Stein Agency

Nadia Anjuman: 'Nazm', translated by Khizra Aslam
published in *MindFire Winter* 2006, by permission of Khizra Aslam

Margaret Atwood: 'A Women's Issue'
from *Eating Fire: Selected Poetry 1965-1995* (Virago Press, 1998). Reproduced with permission of Curtis Brown Group Ltd, London on behalf of Margaret Atwood. © O W Toad Ltd, 1998

Author unknown: 'Dear Fahimeh', translated by Hubert Moore and Nasrin Parvaz
published in *Modern Poetry in Translation*, Third Series Number Four (2005), by permission of Hubert Moore, Nasrin Parvaz and *Modern Poetry in Translation*

Author unknown: 'Rich Woman, Poor Woman'
published in *Sojourners* (July 1985). Reprinted with permission from Sojourners, (800) 714-7474, www.sojo.net

Leila Djabali: 'For My Torturer, Lieutenant D...', translated by Anita Barrows
from *Women Poets of the World* edited by Joanna Bankier and Dierdre
Lashgari (Macmillan,1983), by permission of Anita Barrows

Gevorg Emin: 'Small', translated by Diana Der-Hovanessian
from *For You On New Year's Day: Selected Poems of Gevorg Emin*, edited by
Diana Der-Hovanessian (Ohio University Press, 1986), by permission of Diana
Der-Hovanessian

John Eppel: 'Vendor and Child'
from *Long Time Coming: Short Writings From Zimbabwe*, edited by Jane
Morris ('amaBooks, 2008), by permission of 'amaBooks

Azad Essa: 'We are struggling to understand'
from the Thought Leader blog page of the *Mail & Guardian* online (www.
thoughtleader.co.za/azadessa), 2008, by permission of Azad Essa

Rostislav Evdokimov-Vohac: '... But then again, what's the difference',
translated by Emily D Johnson
published in *World Literature Today*, by permission of Rostislav Evdokimov-
Vohac and Emily D Johnson

Forugh Farrokhzad: 'The Sin', translated by Ahmad Karimi-Hakkak
from *Remembering the Flight* (Nik Publishers, 1997), by permission of
Ahmad Karimi-Hakkak

Zulfikar Ghose: 'Geography Lesson'
from *Jets from Orange* (Macmillan and Co Ltd, 1967), by permission of
Zulfikar Ghose

Luis Enrique Mejía Godoy: 'Revenge', translated by Dinah Livingstone
from *The Nicaraguan Epic* by Carlos & Luis Enrique Mejía Godoy and
Julio Valle-Castillo, translated by Dinah Livingstone (Katabasis, 1989), by
permission of Dinah Livingstone

Lorna Goodison: 'From the Garden of the Women Once Fallen: Thyme'
by permission of Lorna Goodison

Kimiko Hahn: 'These Current Events'
reprinted from *Volatile* ©1999 by Kimiko Hahn, by permission of Hanging
Loose Press

Reesom Haile: 'Desta', translated by Charles Cantalupo
from *We Have Our Voice: Selected Poems of Reesom Haile*, translated by
Charles Cantalupo (The Red Sea Press, Inc., 2000), by permission of Charles
Cantalupo and The Red Sea Press

Laura Hershey: 'You Get Proud by Practicing'
from www.LauraHershey.com, by permission of Laura Hershey

Robert Hershon: 'Calls from the Outside World'
reprinted from *Calls from the Outside World* ©2006 by Robert Hershon, by
permission of Hanging Loose Press

William Heyen: 'Emancipation Proclamation'
from *Pterodactyl Rose: Poems of Ecology* (Time Being Books, 1991), by
William Heyen, reprinted by permission of Time Being Books. © 1991 by
Time Being Press

Rita Ann Higgins: 'Some People'
from *Throw in the Vowels: New & Selected Poems* by Rita Ann Higgins
(Bloodaxe Books, 2005), by permission of Bloodaxe Books

Nazim Hikmet: 'On Living', translated by Randy Blasing and Mutlu Konuk
from *Poems of Nazim Hikmet* (Persea Books, 2002), permission of Persea Books

Antonio S Joquiño, Jr: 'Crocodiles Under the House', translated by Leoncio P
Deriada
published in *Modern Poetry in Translation*, New Series, Number 9 (Summer
1996), by permission of *Modern Poetry in Translation*

Meena Kandasamy: 'Becoming a Brahmin'
from *Touch* (Peacock Books, 2006), by permission of Meena Kandasamy

Orsolya Karafiath: 'Who Gives the Other One?', translated by David A Hill
with Ildikó Juhász
published in *Modern Poetry in Translation* No 21 (2003), by permission of
Modern Poetry in Translation

Ademir Kenović, Abdulah Sidran: from '*Perfect Circle*'
extract appeared in Andrew Horton's article 'Beyond no man's land: comic
tragedy & tearful laughter in cinemas of the Balkans', *World Literature Today*
(October-December 2003)

Kim Sa-In: 'Sleeping on the Street', translated by Brother Anthony of Taizé
from Brother Anthony of Taizé's website http://hompi.sogang.ac.kr/anthony/
NinePoems.htm, by permission of Brother Anthony of Taizé

Kim Sŭng-hŭi: 'Sun Mass', translated by Brother Anthony of Taizé
from *The Columbia Anthology of Modern Korean Poetry* edited by David
McCann (Columbia University Press, 2004), by permission of Brother Anthony
of Taizé and Columbia University Press

Mzi Mahola: 'Impassable Bridge'
from *When Rains Come* (Carapace Poets an imprint of Snailpress, South
Africa, 2000)

Roni Margulies: 'The Slipper', translated by Saliha Paker and Mel Kenne
by permission of Saliha Paker

Rudolf Marku: 'Caligula's Horse'
Visar Zhiti: 'Love', both translated by Robert Elsie
from *An Elusive Eagle Soars: Anthology of Modern Albanian Poetry* edited
and translated by Robert Elsie (Forest Books/UNESCO, 1993), by permission
of Robert Elsie

Jamie McKendrick: 'Il Capitano'
from *Sky Nails. Poems 1979-1997* (Faber, 2000), by permission of Jamie
McKendrick

Larisa Miller: 'Let's fill in the form: date of birth', translated by Richard
McKane
published in *Modern Poetry in Translation*, Number 20 (2002), by
permission of *Modern Poetry in Translation*

Hubert Moore: 'The ultimate rendition'
published in *Modern Poetry in Translation*, Third Series, Number 5 (2006),
by permission of Hubert Moore and *Modern Poetry in Translation*

Yunna Morits: 'A Memory', translated by Daniel Weissbort
published in *Modern Poetry in Translation*, Number 20 (2002), by
permission of *Modern Poetry in Translation*

Fatiha Morchid: 'A Will', translated by Norddine Zouitni
from *Ima'aat* (Dar Attakafah, 2002); translation published on the Morocco
section of Poetry International Web, by permission of Norddine Zouitni

Edison Mpina: 'The Men Next Door'
from *Gathering Seaweed: African Prison Writing* edited by Jack Mapanje
(Heinemann African Writers Series, 2002)

Harryette Mullen: 'We are not responsible'
from *Sleeping with the Dictionary* by Harryette Mullen © 2002 University of
California Press, by permission of University of California Press

H S Venkatesh Murthy: 'Electric Lights Come to Puttalli', translated by A K
Ramanujan
from *The Penguin New Writing in India* edited by Aditya Behl and David
Nichols (Penguin, 1994)

Khalil Mutran: 'Boycott', translated by Issa Boullata and Thomas G Ezzy
from *Modern Arabic Poetry* edited by Salma Khadra Jayyusi (Columbia
University Press, 1987), by permission of Issa Boullata

Taslima Nasrin: 'Character'
appears on taslimanasrin.com, by permission of Taslima Nasrin

Aquiles Nazoa: 'Irregular Verbs', translated by Vanessa Baird
this translation not previously published, by permission of Vanessa Baird

Bino A Realuyo: 'Filipenza'
from *The Gods We Worship Live Next Door* by Bino A Realuyo (University of Utah Press, 2006), by permission of Bino A Realuyo

Rekha: 'Wanderer'
from *Facing the Mirror: Lesbian Writing from India* edited by Ashwini Sukthankar (Penguin Books India, 1999), by permission of Rekha

Adrienne Rich: 'The Eye'
from *The School Among the Ruins: Poems 2000 – 2004* by Adrienne Rich. © 2004 by Adrienne Rich. Used by permission of the author and W. W. Norton & Company, Inc

Michael Rumaker: 'The Fairies Are Dancing All Over the World'
first published and © by Michael Rumaker in *Gay Sunshine*, 1975; subsequent printings 1977, 1983, 1986, 1988, and 2005, by permission of Michael Rumaker

Ken Saro-Wiwa: 'The True Prison'
from *A Month and a Day & Letters by Ken Saro-Wiwa* (Ayebia Clarke Publishing Ltd, 2005), by permission of Ayebia Clarke Publishing Ltd

Saw Wai: 'February 14', translated by David Law
by permission of David Law

Aharon Shabtai: 'Passover 2002', translated by Peter Cole
from *J'Accuse*, © 2002 by Aharon Shabtai, translation © 2002 by Peter Cole, is reprinted by permission of New Directions Publishing, all rights reserved.

Ahmad Shamlu: 'In This Dead-End', translated by Gholam Reza Sami Gorgan Roodi
published in *Modern Poetry in Translation* Number 21 (2003), by permission of *Modern Poetry in Translation*

Siamanto: 'The Dance', translated by Peter Balakian and Nevart Yaghlian
from *Bloody News from My Friend: Poems by Siamanto*, translated by Peter Balakian and Nevart Yaghlian (Wayne State University Press, 1996), by permission of Peter Balakian

Goran Simić: 'A Scene, After the War', translated by Amela Simić
from *Immigrant Blues* by Goran Simić (Brick Books, 2003), by permission of Goran Simić

José Oswald de Andrade Souza: 'Portuguese Mistake', translated by Régis Bonvicino and Douglas Messerli
from *Nothing the Sun could not Explain: 20 Contemporary Brazilian Poets* edited by Michael Palmer, Régis Bonvincino and Nelson Ascher (Sun & Moon Press, Los Angeles, 1997)

Jennifer Strauss: 'The Snapshot Album of the Innocent Tourist'
from *Labour Ward* (Pariah Press, 1988), by permission of Jennifer Strauss

Pireeni Sundaralingam: 'Letters from Exile'
first published in *Cyphers* (2002), by permission of Pireeni Sundaralingam

Wisława Szymborska: 'Psalm', translated by Mark Belletini
published in *New Internationalist*, July 2008, by permission of Mark Belletini

Rowena Torrevillas: 'Thinking With the Body'
published in *Modern Poetry in Translation* New Series, Number 9 (Summer
1996), by permission of *Modern Poetry in Translation* and Rowena
Torrevillas

Solomon Tsehaye: 'The Tithe of War', translated by Charles Cantalupo and
Ghirmai Negash
from *Who Needs a Story? Contemporary Eritrean Poetry in Tigrinya,
Tigre and Arabic* edited by Charles Cantalupo and Ghirmai Negash (Hdri
Publishers, 2005), by permission of Charles Cantalupo, Ghirmai Negash and
Solomon Tsehaye

Tenzin Tsundue: 'Exile House'
by permission of Tenzin Tsundue

U Tin Moe: 'Desert Years', translated by Kyi May Kaung
by permission of Kyi May Kaung

Julio Valle-Castillo: 'Rafaela Padilla', translated by Dinah Livingstone
from *The Nicaraguan Epic* by Carlos & Luis Enrique Mejía Godoy and
Julio Valle-Castillo, translated by Dinah Livingstone (Katabasis, 1989), by
permission of Dinah Livingstone

Christopher van Wyk: 'In Detention'
from *Poets to the People* edited by Barry Feinberg (Mayibuye Books, 1980)

Christopher Whyte: 'Hope (An Dochas)', translated by Christopher Whyte
from *Take Any Train* edited by Peter Daniels (The Oscars Press, 1990), by
permission of Christopher Whyte

Wu Mei: 'The Agreement'
English version by Dinyar Godrej from a Dutch translation by Daan
Bronkhorst

Can Yücel: 'Cradle Rocking', translated by Murat Nemet-Nejat
from *The Penguin Book of Turkish Verse*, edited by Nermin Menemencioğlu
with Fahir İz (Penguin Books, 1978)

Natan Zach: 'On the Desire for Precision', translated by Peter Cole
translation © Peter Cole, by permission of Peter Cole

Ghassan Zaqtan: 'Delighted With My Things', translated by Saadi Simawe and Ellen Doré Watson
published in *Modern Poetry in Translation* Number 14 (Winter 1998-99), by permission of *Modern Poetry in Translation*

Amnesty International

We are all born free and equal in dignity and rights.
Join **Amnesty International** and make a difference.

Amnesty International is a movement of ordinary people standing up for humanity and human rights. Our purpose is to protect individuals wherever justice, fairness, freedom and truth are denied.

With over two million supporters globally, we produce extraordinary results. Prisoners of conscience are released. Death sentences are commuted. Torturers are brought to justice. Governments are persuaded to change their laws and practices. Our achievements have a real impact on people's lives. And your support will make us even stronger.

Amnesty International UK
The Human Rights Action Centre
17-15 New Inn Yard
London EC2A 3EA
tel: 020 7033 1596
email: sct@amnesty.org.uk
www.amnesty.org.uk

New Internationalist

The **New Internationalist** is an independent not-for-profit publishing co-operative. Our mission is to report on issues of world poverty and inequality; to focus attention on the unjust relationship between the powerful and the powerless worldwide; to debate and campaign for the radical changes necessary if the needs of all are to be met.

We publish informative current affairs titles, like the No-Nonsense Guides and the World Changing imprint, complemented by world food, fiction, photography and alternative gift books, as well as calendars and diaries, maps and posters – all with a global justice world view.

We also publish the monthly **New Internationalist** magazine. Each month tackles a subject of global significance, exploring each issue in a concise way which is easy to understand. Feature articles are packed full of photos, charts and graphs and each issue also contains reviews, country profiles, interviews and news.

To find out more about the **New Internationalist**, subscribe to the magazine or buy any of our books take a look at: **www.newint.org**